KU-363-223

A GLOSSARY OF
LANGUAGE AND MIND

TITLES IN THE SERIES INCLUDE

Peter Trudgill
A Glossary of Sociolinguistics
0 7486 1623 3

Laurie Bauer
A Glossary of Morphology
0 7486 1853 8

Alan Davies
A Glossary of Applied Linguistics
0 7846 1854 6

Geoffrey Leech
A Glossary of English Grammar
0 7486 1729 9

A Glossary of
Language and Mind

Jean Aitchison

Edinburgh University Press

© Jean Aitchison, 2003

Edinburgh University Press Ltd
22 George Square, Edinburgh

Typeset in Sabon
by Hewer Text Ltd, Edinburgh, and
printed and bound in Great Britain by
Cox & Wyman Ltd, Reading

A CIP record for this book is
available from the British Library

ISBN 0 7486 1824 4 (paperback)

The right of Jean Aitchison to be
identified as author of this work has
been asserted in accordance with the
Copyright, Designs and Patents Act 1988.

Introduction

Psycholinguistics, the study of language and mind, is the subject which links psychology and linguistics. As one might expect, it is studied by both psychologists and linguists.

Yet these two types of people tackle the topic in different ways. Many psychologists probe into language and mind by carrying out strictly controlled experiments. Linguists, on the other hand, prefer to study speech in naturalistic settings.

Both ways have advantages and disadvantages. The care and control found in psychological experiments guarantees that any result which finds its way into print has been checked out rigorously. But the work of psychologists is bedevilled by the so-called 'experimental paradox': the more carefully controlled the experiment, the more unreal and unnatural the situation, the more likely it is that those being tested have devised one-off strategies for handling a non-natural event. Linguists, meanwhile, guarantee that relatively little is omitted when they explore naturalistic language in natural settings. But the drawback is obvious: cartloads of information are obtainable from almost every sentence. Linguists have to take care not to drown in data. The views of both psychologists and linguists, therefore, need to be considered and amalgamated.

Psycholinguistics is a subject which has expanded dramatically in the last fifty years. In the first half of the twientieth century it was a minor topic of interest to a few psychologists, who looked mostly at single words, and how they might be linked to others. But it has now become a major sub-discipline within both psychology and linguistics. It sprawls in all directions. Just as a street market which once sold vegetables might expand into having stalls for meat, flowers, books, even second-hand furniture, so psycholinguistics has turned itself into a vast academic hypermarket which has imported goods from a number of other disciplines.

The core topics within psycholinguistics are comprehension (how people understand speech), production (how humans produce speech) and acquisition (how children learn language). These branches of the subject burgeoned in the 1960s. In recent years psycholinguistics has been supplemented by information on language and the brain (neurolinguistics), on speech disorders (clinical linguistics, aphasiology), on the dictionary in the brain (the mental lexicon), and on animal communication (which explores to what extent other species either naturally have some of the properties of human language, or are able to acquire them). Psycholinguistics has also been influenced by the new, interdisciplinary area of cognitive science – an amalgam of linguistics, psychology, philosophy and artifical intelligence.

In the first half of the twentieth century, psycholinguistics was a minor topic which primarily looked at individual words, and tried to find out which ones might be closely associated, as with *sister* and *brother*, *husband* and *wife*, *rose* and *flower*.

But then it all changed. 1959 is sometimes taken as the starting point of the modern era of psycholinguistics. That year, the linguist Noam Chomsky published a highly critical review of a book, *Verbal behavior* (1957) written by the prominent behaviourist B. F. Skinner. Behaviorist psychologists claimed that all learning was a case of breaking the learning down into very small steps, and repeatedly rewarding the learner. This had proved effective in the training of rats and pigeons. Skinner argued that the procedure could be extended to humans learning language. But in a witty and devastating review, Chomsky argued that rats learning how to press levers

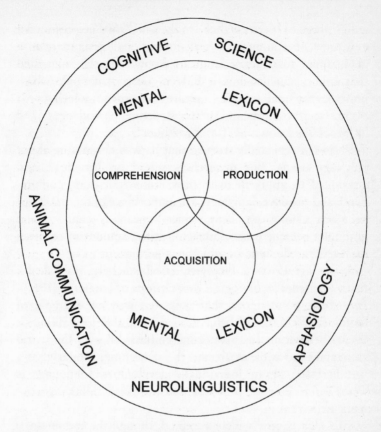

Fig. 1 Psycholinguistics

to get food could not be compared to humans acquiring language, which is far more complex. Chomsky suggested that, far from being an accumulation of simple steps, language was a unique, specialised skill: humans might be innately programmed to talk, he asserted, a viewpoint that is now widely accepted. This heady suggestion was the yeast which made the dough of psycholinguistics rise and expand.

Chomsky himself was concerned primarily with abstract linguistic knowledge or 'competence' rather than actual language usage or 'performance'. In the late 1950s he proposed a new type of grammar, a 'transformational' grammar, as a groundplan for human language knowledge. He suggested that every sentence has a hidden 'deep structure', which underlies the final 'surface structure', the order in which words occur. Deep structure and surface structure, he said, are linked by processes known as 'tranformations'.

Chomsky repeatedly warned that he was not talking about language usage. But researchers seized on his ideas, and attempted to apply them to how humans acquire, comprehend, and produce, language. The importance of this era is not so much Chomsky's ideas, which repeatedly changed and gradually became more abstract, but the amount of research they generated, some of which has permanent value.

In the late 1960s, a biologist, Eric Lenneberg, published a book entitled *The biological foundations of language* (1967). Lenneberg pointed out that language was an example of biologically controlled behaviour, comparable to walking or sexual behaviour. Just as normal children all over the world sit, stand, and walk at around the same time, similarly, at a certain stage in an individual's development, language is scheduled to emerge, provided that the surrounding environment is normal.

This idea is now widely accepted, though the terminology has changed. Nowadays, researchers talk about 'innately guided learning'. Children, by nature, have a broad general notion of how to tackle the sounds they hear coming out of people's mouths, and how to organise them into a layered 'grammar'.

The realisation that language is innately guided triggered an immense amount of careful work on how children build up knowledge of their language. Youngsters' utterances were collected and analysed, and later, so were the utterances of their parents, to see how much parents and children influenced one another. The upshot is that children turn out to be active puzzle solvers. They have inherited an understanding that the sounds coming out of people's mouths are worth listening to, and that it is their task to make sense of them. They instinctively know how to figure out the structure of their language, just as songbirds intuitively learn how to sing.

The tidal wave of enthusiasm for psycholinguistics engulfed mature speech as well. Studies of speech comprehension were mostly carried out on adults. Understanding language turned out to be a mixture of knowledge and guesswork. Humans, when listening to a flow of words, could not be taking down a mental dictation; speech is just too fast. And the sounds are too varied: each speech sound is different depending on its place in a word, and who is saying it. Instead, listeners hear a few bits and pieces, and then jump to conclusions, based on their knowledge of the language they are hearing.

Humans actively consider several possible interpretations as they hear a word or group of words, before they make a final decision. The possible words behave as if they were horses competing against one another in a race. This competition happens in a fraction of a second – so fast and subconsciously that hearers are often unaware that they are considering several possibilities before they make their decision.

Producing speech is also a complex process. Again, words and structures appear to compete against one another like horses, and sometimes end up in a dead heat. Then they can get jumbled up together, as in *buggage*: the speaker meant to say either *baggage* or *luggage*, and somehow said both. Such 'slips of the tongue' can provide valuable information about the hidden stages of speech production.

All in all, far more is going on in the mind than anyone ever realised. The brain is a buzzing hive of activity, as is confirmed by brain scans. But interpretation of the scans is proving a challenge to researchers: even simple repetition of a heard word involves a huge amount of electrical activity in different brain areas.

The area covered by language and mind has therefore grown from a narrow stream to a flooding river, with multiple books and an ever-expanding vocabulary.

This is where this Glossary can help. The Glossary can be used in two ways: first as a simple dictionary, when someone reading another book comes across a term unknown to them, such as, say, *bootstrapping*, *dysarthria*, *neoteny*, *parameter setting*. The term will be explained, and the reader directed to related entries. Second, the Glossary can be used for browsing. Some of the headings are broad outline ones, such as *speech comprehension*. This entry gives the main subcomponents of this process, which can then be looked up. An extensive system of cross-referencing then refers the reader to other connected topics. In order to avoid frustrating the reader too much, there is a certain amount of overlap in the entries. This allows many entries to be complete in themselves, even though ideally the reader will want to gain further information by checking the cross-references.

But this brief book can provide only a glimpse of the complexities involved in learning and using speech. At the end of the Glossary, an annotated bibliography is given, with reading suggestions, in the hope that readers will want to press on and find out more about language and the mind. The book is a revised, updated and expanded version of the author's *Introducing Language and Mind* (Penguin 1992).

A

a-/an- A prefix of Greek origin, meaning 'without'. It is found in the name of several language disorders, where it usually means 'having severe difficulties with'. For example, **aphasia** is literally 'without speech', but normally means 'with serious speech problems'. Similarly, **alexia** literally 'without reading', **agraphia** 'without writing', **anomia** 'without naming ability', **anarthria** 'without muscular control'. These all mean 'severe difficulties with' rather than total lack. In some cases, the prefix *a-* is used interchangeably with terms beginning with *dys-* 'difficulty with', as in **anarthria/dysarthria**, though mostly either the *a-* term or the *dys-* term has won out over the other, as in **aphasia** for speech disorders, and **dyslexia** for reading disorders. Nowadays, some writers use *a-* for acquired disorders (those that occur as a result of damage in the course of life) and *dys-* for developmental or congenital ones (those in which the ability has never developed). (See also **acquired disability.**)

access route vs linguistic representation The route to a word which a person is trying to identify or find (access process) may differ, according to some psycholinguists, from the way that word is represented linguistically in the mind.

acoustic variance Different patterns in the sound waves associated with a single speech sound. A sound such as [p] is likely to vary considerably, depending on the sounds around it, the care with which it was said, and the person who said it. It is therefore said to be 'acoustically variant'. This variability is one reason why **speech perception** is a complex process. (See also **speech comprehension**.)

acquired disability A handicap which arises as a result of damage during a person's lifetime. It is contrasted with the term *developmental disability*, which indicates a condition of unknown origin, which may have been predestined from birth. Someone who experiences reading difficulties as the result of a stroke would have *acquired dyslexia*, whereas a child who had never been able to learn to read normally would have *developmental dyslexia*. A disability which was definitely present at birth is sometimes referred to as a *congenital disability*.

acquired dyslexia see **acquired disability; dyslexia**

acquisition (of language) Mastery of language. *Acquisition vs learning* is considered to be an important distinction by those who think that child language acquisition differs in nature from adult language learning: they argue that adults are exposed to language outside a **critical period** set aside by nature for acquiring language. However, recent research has thrown doubt on a fixed 'critical period', and suggests that it might be more accurate to speak of a **sensitive period**: a time when children are particularly 'tuned in' to acquiring language, and which gradually diminishes in strength. *Acquisition vs emergence* is a distinction between complete mastery of a linguistic structure versus its first appearance. For example, intermittent plural forms in -*s* (*cats, bees*) may emerge several months before plural endings are reliably acquired, with acquisition usually measured as their occurrence in ninety per cent of the places where an adult would expect them. (See also **sensitive period, child language**.)

acquisition vs emergence see **acquisition (of language)**

acquisition vs learning see **acquisition (of language)**

actor-action-object strategy see **canonical sentoid strategy**

agrammatic aphasia A speech disorder in which a patient's ability to produce linguistic structures is seriously impaired. Typically, the patient has considerable difficulty in producing speech, and utters mainly content words (those which contain meaning) with hardly any word endings, and with very little linking them together: *Bed . . . ah . . . Peter come . . . night*. Such a patient is usually able to comprehend speech fairly well. According to some researchers, the patient really knows the grammar, but has difficulty in remembering the form of the 'little words' involved. However, many patients have other problems as well, including some (minor) comprehension difficulties. A complicating factor is that people with agrammatic symptoms sometimes have different underlying disorders. The condition is also known as *Broca's aphasia*, and is often associated with damage to anterior (front) portions of the brain, particularly a location known as Broca's area. (See also **aphasia; Broca's area; localisation**.)

agraphia see **dysgraphia**

AI see **artificial intelligence**

Alex The name of a grey parrot who has learned a certain amount of language. At one time, all birds were thought to be 'bird-brained' and incapable of anything more than 'parrotting' (repetition). But Alex can correctly label more than thirty objects (grape, key, chair, etc), a number of colours and several shapes. He can also respond to questions asking whether colours and shapes are the same or different.

alexia see **dyslexia**

Alzheimer's disease see **DAT**

ambiguity The possession of more than one possible meaning. This can be subdivided into *lexical ambiguity*, when a single word can have more than one meaning, as in *The detective examined the log* (fallen tree or record of a ship's voyage?), and *structural ambiguity*, when the arrangement of words gives rise to more than one interpretation. The latter is sometimes subdivided: *surface structure ambiguity* is said to occur when the words can be grouped in different ways, as in *hot soup and pies*. Is it *hot* [*soup and pies*], with both items of food heated up? Or *hot soup* [and pies], with the pies remaining cold? *Deep structure ambiguity* is said to occur when the source of the ambiguity is less easily identifiable, as in *The duck was ready to eat*. Is the duck about to eat or be eaten? Ambiguous words and structures are important for the information they can potentially provide about the way in which humans comprehend sentences. Research indicates that humans may briefly notice all common meanings of an ambiguous word, even though they are not consciously aware of doing so, then discard the unwanted ones. There is less agreement over the treatment of structural ambiguity. Some researchers argue that hearers notice only one meaning, and then retrace their steps if they have made a mistake and been led 'up the garden path'. Others argue for a brief consideration of more than one interpretation, even though hearers might not realise they are doing this. (See also **garden-path sentences**; **perceptual strategies**; **speech comprehension**.)

American Sign Language see **sign language**

Ameslan (American Sign Language, ASL) see **sign language**

analysis-by-synthesis see **motor theory (of speech perception)**

anarthria An inability to speak caused by muscular weakness. The term is sometimes used interchangeably with *dysarthria*, which in theory is less severe. Anarthria is commonly associated with other physical symptoms such as difficulty in chewing and swallowing. The central speech processes are normally intact, and the patient is simply unable to pronounce the speech which he or she has planned, as sometimes occurs in sufferers from Parkinson's disease. (See also **a-/an-**.)

animal communication The natural systems by which non-human animate beings convey information to one another. This may be via sound (dolphins, birds), sight (sticklebacks), touch (ants), or smell (moths). The interest of these systems lies in their similarities to and differences from human language. Human language contains several **design features** which are rare or non-existent in animal communication: most notable of these are **creativity** (ability to produce novel utterances), **displacement** (ability to refer to objects and events removed in time and space) and **structure dependence** (the presence of internal structure). There is a **continuity vs discontinuity** dispute between researchers. Some argue that human language developed out of an earlier animal system. Others claim that it is totally different. Natural animal communication systems need to be kept distinct from attempts to teach signs to apes based on human languages. (See also **ape signing; bee dancing; delphinology.**)

anomia Severe word-finding problems, literally 'without naming ability'. This is common in all types of **aphasia** (speech disorders). It occurs in a mild form in almost everybody, and usually gets worse as a person gets older. The **TOT** ('tip-of-the-tongue') **phenomenon** is the well-known feeling that an elusive word is 'on the tip of one's tongue'. Experimental studies of this have provided some insight into how people find the words they want when producing speech (**word retrieval**). (See also **speech production.**)

anticipation error The premature (too early) insertion of a sound, syllable, word or sign when speaking, reading, writing or signing. For example: *There's a shalt . . . salt shortage*; *It's amazingly how quickly people pick these things up*; *Unwieldy people . . . unscrupulous people can wield too much power*. Such **slips of the tongue** (speech errors) are important, because of the information they provide about the process of **speech production**. Anticipations are **assemblage errors**, in that the correct items have been selected, but then wrongly assembled, as opposed to **selection errors**, where a wrong choice has been made. Anticipations are the commonest type of assemblage error. They suggest that speech is planned some way in advance of being uttered. They also give clues as to the size of the chunks which are pre-prepared. Similar information is given by anticipations in reading, writing and signing. (See also **slip of the eye; slip of the hand; speech production.**)

antiphonal singing Alternate singing by some species of birds: one sings, then stops and waits for the other to take its turn. This has some similarities to **turn-taking** in human conversation.

ape signing The use by chimps and related species of a simplified variety of the sign language used by deaf people in the US (American Sign Language, or ASL). Starting in the 1960s, a number of American researchers have attempted to teach various apes a language-like system, in order to see whether the properties of language were easily handled by animals, or whether they were unique to humans. These animals, of whom the most famous were the chimps **Washoe** and **Nim Chimpsky**, each acquired around 200 signs. They could name people and common objects, request absent foods and playthings, and could combine signs in a limited way. However, most of them displayed excitable, repetitive signing, sometimes using both hands at once. None of them has shown evidence of reliable structure in their output, suggesting that their system lacks **structure dependence**. Other chimps were taught to manipulate prepared tokens, of whom the most famous are **Lana** and **Kanzi** (a bonobo). Both of these use a keyboard. (See also **sign language**.)

aphasia Any serious speech disorder which involves basic language processes. Such a condition is commonly caused by an accident or a stroke (known technically as a CVA: cerebro-vascular accident). In British English, the term, 'aphasia' (literally 'lack of speech') used to be reserved for serious problems, and the term 'dysphasia' was applied to more trivial ones. Nowadays, the term 'aphasia' usually covers both, following American usage. Aphasia is studied in the hope that speech disorders might provide information about the way in which the human mind copes with language: if some aspects of language are damaged, and others left intact, then it might be possible to identify various independent linguistic components within the brain/mind. There are several recognisable types of aphasia, of which the best known are **agrammatic** or **Broca's aphasia**, **fluent** or **Wernicke's aphasia**, and **conduction aphasia**. In addition, the broad term **expressive aphasia** is sometimes used for disorders affecting speech production, and **receptive aphasia** for those involving speech comprehension. Various controversial attempts have been made to link these aphasias with specific areas in the brain (**localisation**). However, damage is rarely restricted to one small area, especially as the locations near it are often either starved of blood, or flooded with it. Consequently, many patients present symptoms which seem to indicate a combination of aphasia types. The study of aphasia is known as *aphasiology*. (See also **a-/an-**.)

aphasiology see **aphasia**

arcuate fasciculus A bundle of nerve fibres in the brain which connect **Broca's area** with **Wernicke's area**. (See **localisation of language**.)

argument structure The structure attached to verbs, which in English usually follows verbs. In the sentence 'Penelope gave milk to the cat', the last four words form the 'argument', a term borrowed from some types of logic. The need to include an argument in a sentence may explain why those suffering from **agrammatic aphasia** find verbs harder to handle than nouns.

artificial intelligence (AI) Attempts to model the mental ability of human beings on computers. One important way in which discoveries about human abilities can be made is to attempt to make a simplified 'model' of the processes involved. This involves breaking down the ability into step-by-step procedures, and then writing a computer program which, ideally, replicates them. In the area of language, AI has mostly been applied to comprehension. Computers find it hard to deal with the type of ambiguity routinely handled by humans, such as: *Bill watched the owl with binoculars*. English-speaking humans would know immediately that it is Bill, rather than the owl who has the binoculars, but the computer would find it hard to select the correct solution. (See also **computational linguistics; connectionism; speech comprehension**.)

ASL (American Sign Language) see **sign language**

assemblage error A mistake in which sounds, syllables, words or signs have been put together in the wrong order in speaking, writing, or signing. These misorderings are of three main types: **anticipations** (premature insertion), as in *she shells* 'sea shells', **exchanges** or *transpositions* (place-swapping), as in *cling spreaning* 'spring cleaning', and **perseverations** (repetitions), as in *one-way woad* 'one-way road'. Such errors provide important information about the way humans prepare and produce speech: for example, the large number of anticipations, compared with perseverations, indicates that humans are thinking ahead as they speak, and are able to erase the memory of what they have said quite fast. Assemblage errors contrast with **selection errors**, in which a wrong item has been chosen. Together, these form the two major subdivisions within **slips of the tongue** (speech errors). A similar distinction can be made within **slips of the pen** (writing errors), and **slips of the hand** (signing errors). (See also **anticipation error; exchange error; perseveration error; speech production**.)

ATN (Augmented Transition Network) A partial model of language comprehension widely adopted by early researchers in artificial intelligence. It attempted to simulate **parsing**, the assignment of structure to groups of words. Basically, this was a 'top-down' model, which set up expectations, and then checked to see if these were fulfilled. For example, it might contain the instruction 'Start out by looking for a NOUN PHRASE', and would then search for a DETERMINER – ADJECTIVE – NOUN sequence, such as *the old pig*. It was never a wholly realistic model of human comprehension, partly because if it went wrong, it always had to backtrack (go back and start again). But attempts to model sentence comprehension can provide useful pointers to the ways in which humans understand language. (See also **artificial intelligence; connectionism; model; parsing; speech comprehension; top-down vs bottom-up processing.**)

auditory cortex The section of the brain which deals with hearing. (See also **brain; localisation of language.**)

automatic speech Speech sequences that have been so well practised that they do not require any conscious effort, and are retained even in some cases of **aphasia**. Such a routine takes up relatively little processing time.

B

babbling A technical term which describes the sounds made by babies when they produce repeated syllables such as *ba-ba-ba*, *ma-ma-ma*, *da-da-da*, The babbling stage follows an earlier **cooing** (*goo-goo*) stage, and starts when the infant is about six months old. Babbling sounds are mostly ones which are physically easy to produce, usually those made fairly far forward in the mouth. The purpose of babbling may be to allow the baby to strengthen and gain control over the vocal organs which will be used later in speech. Babbling is normally meaningless, although parents often assume that the child is referring to them, which is why the words *papa* and *mama* , or similar, are so widespread in the world as names for parents. Some early reports suggested that babies babbled every possible sound, but this turned out to be a myth, as the sounds babbled are in fact fairly restricted. In addition, there seems to be a *babbling drift*, in that a baby's babbles gradually move closer to the sounds found in the language around. Babbling continues for some months, and in most children, it overlaps with their first words. An earlier report that there was a gap between babbling and speech turned out to be false. Babies acquiring tone languages, where words are distinguished by the pitch of the voice, as in Chinese, reportedly babble somewhat differently from babies acquiring English. (See also **child language**.)

babbling drift see **babbling**

baby-talk see **caregiver language**

basic level category The level at which a visual image can be most readily formed. For example, *dog*, *chair*, are basic level categories. *Poodle* and *armchair* are lower and more specific, and *animal* and *furniture* are higher, and more general.

bathtub effect A description sometimes given to the well-known finding that people remember the beginnings and ends of words better than the middle, as if the word were a person lying in a bathtub with their head out of the water at one end, and their feet out at the other, as with *emanate* for 'emulate', *confusion* for 'conclusion'.

bee dancing Body movements of bees by which they inform other bees of the location of nectar-bearing flowers. It is of interest for language, because bees can communicate about nectar sources which are out of sight, so their system has the property of **displacement**, which is rare among animals. But bee dancing is unlike human language in that it is limited to discussing nectar in certain restricted ways, so it is not **creative**. (See also **animal communication; creativity; design features.**)

behaviourism A movement in psychology, whose supporters argued that human behaviour could be shaped by reinforcement (rewards). The primary aim of behaviourists was to predict and control human behaviour without speculation about internal mental states. The movement became important for language primarily as a result of a book *Verbal behavior* (1957) by the American B. F. Skinner, in which he claimed that procedures used to train rats and pigeons were applicable to the development of language in humans. He was heavily criticised for this by the American linguist Noam **Chomsky** (1928–), on the grounds that Skinner had failed to understand the basic nature of language, especially its **creativity** (ability to handle an indefinite number of novel utterances). Chomsky's review (1959) of Skinner's book is regarded as a turning point in the study of **innateness**, the claim that language might be genetically programmed in humans. (See also **design features; operant conditioning.**)

big dictionary effect The observation that in studies of vocabulary size, usually based on testing people on a controlled sample of a dictionary (such as the first word at the top of each page), the result varies according to the size of the dictionary: the bigger the dictionary, the more words people appear to know.

bilingualism The ability to speak two languages. At one time, it was claimed that there were two types of bilinguals, *compound bilinguals*, whose languages were intermingled in the mind, and *co-ordinate bilinguals*, whose languages were kept as separate systems. This oversimple theory is now regarded as outmoded, as most people seem to fluctuate, depending on the type of task being tested. Children who are brought up bilingual or *multilingual* (speaking several languages) sometimes lag behind monolingual children in the early stages of development, but they quickly catch up, and normally become proficient in both or all the languages at an early age.

biologically controlled behaviour see **maturationally controlled behaviour**

bioprogram A controversial view put forward by the linguist Derek Bickerton that an innate blueprint known as the 'bioprogram' caused certain basic distinctions (such as a difference between 'before' and 'not before') to appear at the origin of language, and causes them to appear in creoles (newly-formed languages), and in child language.

birdsong The melodies sung by birds, in contrast to bird calls. Some birds have a system of simple calls including, for example, an alarm call, and a 'gathering' call alongside a more elaborate system involving melodies. This has led some people to compare birds with humans, who may have a similar twofold means of communication, with a system of cries seen in babies, and an elaborate superimposed language. Birdsong has some other similarities with human language: each note becomes meaningful only when placed alongside other notes, much as human sounds need to be strung together to form words. Birdsong, like human language, is controlled primarily by one side of the brain, and the song of some birds also involves a certain amount of learning. Consequently, birdsong is sometimes claimed to be the animal communication system which is nearest to human language. However, it is unlike language in that birdsong can possibly only convey messages about mating and territorial rights, so is not truly **creative** (able to handle an indefinite number of novel utterances). (See also **animal communication; creativity; design features.**)

blend An error in which two words or phrases are combined into one, in speaking, writing, reading or signing. For example: *climbered* (climbed + clambered), *sittle down* (sit + settle down), *off his mind* (off his rocker + out of his mind). Blends, like other **slips of the tongue** (speech errors), provide important information about how humans prepare and produce utterances. Blends are **selection errors**, in which a mistake has been made in the choice of item, as opposed to **assemblage errors**, in which correctly selected items have been misordered. Many blends involve words with similar meaning, suggesting that the speaker has mentally activated both, then been unable to decide which to select. *Telescopic blends* are those in which syllables or words have been omitted, as in *foreigncy* (foreign currency), *sprinkling* (spring cleaning), which sometimes happen when people's speech plans run ahead of their actual utterance. Blends within **slips of the pen** (writing errors) and **slips of the hand** (signing errors) provide similar information about writing and signing. (See also **speech production.**)

blind children see **Kelli**

blocking The common frustrating experience of being unable to think of a required word because another similar in sound or meaning 'blocks' access to the one being sought. For example, the flower *gladioli* has been reported as blocking *amaryllis*, and the word *accelerate* was noted to block *escalate*.

bloodflow patterns (in the brain) see **brain scans**

BNC see **British National Corpus**

bonobo see **ape signing; Kanzi**

bootstrapping (booting) A process by which a computer is started up, which involves using a simple program before it can proceed to a more complex one. This metaphor has also been applied to children acquiring language over the problem of how they 'break into' the language system. A *bootstrapping approach* suggests that they start with a simple system, perhaps one which relies heavily on meaning: an utterance *Polly shoe* 'Polly's shoe' might initially be regarded as a formula expressing possession. At a later stage, the child would realise that the sequence fitted the same 'slot' in a sentence as other phrases such as *pretty birdie*. Then he or she would gradually move away from such strong reliance on the meaning, and would start to analyse phrases as linguistic structures, rather than meaning-based formulae. (See also **child language; two-word stage.**)

bootstrapping approach see **bootstrapping**

brain The portion of the central nervous system enclosed within the skull, which controls both unconscious reflexes and conscious thought in vertebrates (animals with backbones). The human brain can be divided into two main sections, a lower *brainstem*, whose task it is to keep the human alive, and a higher *cerebrum* which intregrates humans with their environment. The cerebrum is divided into two *cerebral hemispheres*, of which the left hemisphere is usually the dominant one, and the most important for language. The hemispheres are joined by various bridges or commissures of which the most important is the *corpus callosum*. The deeply folded outer layer of the brain is known as the *cerebral cortex* (from the Latin word for 'skin', 'rind'), and is made up of billions of nerve cells or *neurons* which are grey in colour once a person is dead. This gives rise to the colloquial phrase 'Use your grey matter' for 'Think!' – though in live patients the brain is in fact pink. The front portions of the brain are referred to as 'anterior', and the back portions as 'posterior'. For greater precision, each hemisphere is divided into four *lobes* (frontal, parietal, temporal, occipital) (Fig. 2), and any brain location can be expressed even more accurately by specifying its fold or *convolution*. For example, the third frontal convolution may be important for language production. (See **brain scans; brain vs mind;**

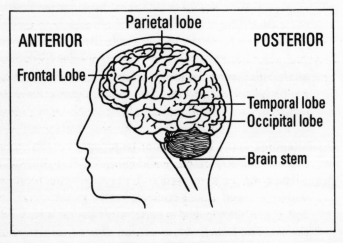

ANTERIOR

Parietal lobe

POSTERIOR

Frontal Lobe

Temporal lobe
Occipital lobe

Brain stem

Fig. 2   The brain

cerebral dominance; localisation of language; neurolinguistics; split brain.)

brain–body ratio Brain weight in proportion to body weight. Human brains are relatively heavy in relation to body weight, leading to suggestions that this could be related to language. But neither absolute weights, nor relative weights of brains and bodies is thought to be crucial. Brain–body weight ratios have been found to be similar for a three-year-old chimp, a thirteen-year-old boy, and a twelve-year-old male dwarf, of which the last two can talk, but the first cannot. Brain organisation is therefore more important for language than brain size.

brain scans Brain scans map bloodflow in the brain, which can shed light on speech processing. Blood surges when a brain area is active, and this can show which areas of the brain are being used when people are asked to perform simple language tasks. Nouns show different bloodflow patterns from verbs, and regular verbs show different flow-patterns from irregular ones.

brainstem see **brain**

brain vs mind The physical organ in the skull which controls bodily behaviour and thought, in contrast to the various intellectual and emotional capabilities of humans. Ideally, these two would be closely connected. In practice, the workings of the brain cannot be directly correlated with human thought, language and emotion, though **neurolinguistics** attempts to find links between the brain and language, and *neuropsychology* attempts to find links between the brain and mental activities in general. **Psycholinguistics** is the general name for the study of language and mind.

British National Corpus A database of real language samples, both spoken and written. Such a database enables detailed research into speech patterns to be carried out, and has shown, for example, that connections between words which habitually occur together are very strong, as in *bread and butter*, *knife and fork*. This may explain why people find it easy to remember opposites, which are often found together, such as *hot and cold*, *open and shut*.

British Sign Language see **sign language**

Broca's aphasia see **agrammatic aphasia**

Broca's area An area of the brain named after the French neurologist Paul Broca, who identified it as important for the production of speech. In 1861, Broca gave an address to the Anthropological Society of Paris, noting that a patient of his who had been unable to produce any speech apart from the sound sequence [tæn] had, in an autopsy, been shown to have serious damage in the left side of the brain, fairly far forward (technically, in the third frontal convolution). He therefore claimed that he had located 'the faculty of articulate language'. This discovery was complemented by that of Wernicke later in the century, who claimed to have found another area important for speech understanding. Since that time, there has been considerable controversy as to whether Broca's area is, or is not, important for speech planning and production. Statistically, an area somewhat similar to that defined by Broca does seem to be important, but brain areas do not seem to be located as reliably as body organs, so the question has still not been finally solved. (See also **brain; localisation; Wernicke's area.**)

BSL (British Sign Language) see **sign language**

$\boxed{C}$

canonical sentoid strategy A short cut or 'strategy' which speakers of languages with a fixed word order apply when they comprehend sentences. They commonly assume that any potential 'sentoid' (sentence-like structure) fits in with the standard or 'canonical' form, which in English is NOUN PHRASE – VERB – (NOUN PHRASE), as in *The duchess sneezed*, *The owl caught a mouse*. This tendency is so strong, that English speakers often find it hard to comprehend sentences such as: *The dog walked past the gorilla collapsed*. This sentence leads many listeners 'up the garden path', since it tends at first to be interpreted as 'the dog walked past, the gorilla collapsed', though on reflection it must be 'The dog which was walked past the gorilla collapsed'. Some researchers have claimed that the canonical sentoid strategy is a special case of a broader comprehension strategy, the **principle of minimal attachment**. (See also **garden-path sentences; minimal attachment; perceptual strategies; speech comprehension.**)

caregiver language The language spoken to children by the people who look after them, also known as *caretaker language*, *motherese*, *baby-talk* and *CDL* (child-directed language). In general, such language is spoken slowly and clearly, at a fairly high pitch, with strong intonation patterns. It also tends to focus on the 'here and now'. These features enable children to split up the stream of speech into smaller units. Most cultures adapt their language when addressing children, though the extent to which they do this varies. The use of made-up 'baby-words' such as *gee-gee*, *moo-cow*, *baa-lamb* seems to be characteristic of English speakers, and is not particularly widespread around the world. Caregiver language has relatively little immediate effect on children, in that intensive coaching on one particular word ending is unlikely to alter a child's behaviour. Even **expansions** (expanded versions of children's utterances produced by adults) are thought to be less useful than **recasts** (saying the same thing in a new way). The main role of caregiver language is to provide clear evidence from which children can extract language in their own way, and at their own speed. (See **child language**.)

caretaker language see **caregiver language**

categorical perception The ability of humans to place a sound firmly into a particular category. If humans are played an artificial sound which is intermediate between [b] and [p], for example, they always say they have heard either [b] or [p], even though there will be differences of opinion as to which they have heard. Some people argue that this shows that human hearing has been specially adapted for dealing with speech sounds. (See also **speech perception**.)

CDL (child-directed language) see **caregiver language**

centre-embedded sentences Sentences in which one or more sentence-like structures are inserted in the middle of another. For example: *The boat [the shark hit] sank* has the sequence *the shark hit* embedded inside *The boat sank*. *The boat [the shark [the fisherman harpooned] hit] sank* has the sequence *the fisherman harpooned* embedded inside *the shark hit*, which is itself embedded inside *The boat sank*. More than one embedding is difficult for humans to understand, so a number of experiments have tried to probe into the source of the difficulty. Finding out why some structures are easier for humans to handle than others is a useful way of finding out how people normally comprehend sentences. (See also canonical sentoid strategy; parsing; perceptual strategies; speech comprehension.)

cerebral cortex see **brain**

cerebral dominance The supremacy of one of the two cerebral hemispheres (halves) of the brain over the other. In most human beings, this is the left. This is due partly to the fact that language is usually controlled by the left hemisphere, and also to right-handedness being the norm, since the left hemisphere controls the right side of the body. (See also **brain; lateralisation; localisation.**)

cerebral hemispheres see **brain**

cerebrum see **brain**

chain complex A view of children's early word meaning proposed by the Russian psychologist Vygotsky (1893–1934). In his view, meanings were often 'chained' onto one another by association. A famous example is the word *qua*, possibly originally the word *quack*, to label a duck swimming on a pond. The liquid element caught the child's attention, so *qua* was next applied to a cup of milk. Yet the duck had not been forgotten, so *qua* was then used to refer to a coin with an eagle on it, and then finally for a teddy bear's eye – possibly linked to the roundness of the coin.

chatterbox syndrome A rare condition in which a flow of speech is produced by children of exceptionally low intelligence. They are sometimes known as 'cocktail party chatterers' (not to be confused with the **cocktail party effect**), since like guests at cocktail parties, they appear to talk for the sake of talking, though their output makes little sense. Laura, an American teenager, produced sentences such as: 'I was sixteen last year, and now I'm nineteen this year', 'It was no regular school, it was just good old no buses'. She was not just repeating phrases she had learned from others, because she produced some grammatical errors she is unlikely to have ever heard, such as: 'Three tickets were gave out by a police last year'.

checklist view of meaning A phrase used by the linguist Charles Fillmore to describe an old view of meaning, which listed the supposed essential meaning components of a word (the 'necessary and sufficient conditions'), and checked them off one by one. A *bachelor* might be described as MALE, SINGLE, UNMARRIED, for example. This view of meaning was realised to be unrealistic, and was replaced in the 1970s by more psychologically plausible theories, such as **prototype theory**.

child language The linguistic output of children, which differs from that of adults. Children do not simply imitate their carers, as is shown by utterances such as *Me drinked tea*, *No teddy go*, which could not have been copied from an adult. Instead, they devise their own language 'rules', which they modify as they get older. There is considerable controversy as to how children formulate these rules. Many people now believe that youngsters are guided by innate linguistic principles, and that language is **maturationally controlled**: it is behaviour which is biologically programmed to emerge at a particular time, provided the environment is normal. This is likely, because there are strong similarities in the language development of widely separated children. More generally, many people now believe that language involves **guided learning,** in which humans are guided in particular directions by inbuilt intuitions – though whether child language development is truly separate from other mental abilities is still under discussion. The timetable below is a typical one for an English-speaking child:

6 weeks	Cooing
6 months	Babbling
8 months	Intonation patterns
12–15 months	Single words
18 months	Two-word utterances
21 months	Three-and-more word utterances
18 months	Simple negatives
18 months	Simple questions
2 years	Inflections (word endings)
3 years	Adult-type negatives
3 years	Adult-type questions
3 years	Adult-type inflections
10 years	Adult-type grammar

(See **acquisition; babbling; caregiver language; cooing; crying; guided learning; innateness; Language Acquisition Device; learnability problem; maturationally controlled behaviour; nature vs nurture controversy; order of acquisition; parameter setting; sensitive period; telegraphic speech.**)

chimpanzees see **ape signing**

Chomksy, A. N. (1928–) American linguist, viewed by many as the most important influence on linguistics in the twentieth century. (Avram) Noam Chomsky is particularly associated with the notion of innateness, the claim that a human's knowledge of language is largely genetically inbuilt, and separate from other cognitive abilities. His views on this innate contribution have changed over the years. His earlier proposals for a **Language Acquisition Device** have been replaced by a suggestion that children are preprogrammed with a knowledge of **Universal Grammar** (UG). This involves understanding some basic linguistic principles, and being aware in advance of some crucial options available to human languages. Children check these possibilities out against the evidence they hear around them in order to choose those consistent with their particular language, and so 'set the parameters' of their internal grammars. Such a model is known as a P & P (**principles and parameters**) model. In his recent work, he has become more concerned with specifying the nature of the human language system in general, in which his **minimalist program** specifies the bare bones, the outline nature of human language, rather than the details of any individual language (See also **innateness; minimalist program; parameter setting.**)

click experiments A procedure used in psycholinguistic experiments in which a person is asked to report the location in a sentence of a sound played during its production. Typically, the hearer is asked to wear headphones, and a 'click' (usually a burst of 'white noise') is played into one ear, and a sentence into the other. Hearers are often somewhat inaccurate in their reports, apparently influenced by the structure of the sentence. Such experiments are therefore sometimes used as evidence for how people assign structure to groups of words when they comprehend sentences. (See also **experimental psycholinguistics; parsing.**)

cocktail party effect The ability of humans to pick out and listen to a particular conversation, even when at a noisy party. This contrasts with the failure of any hearing aid or speech recognition device to do the same. (This phenomenon should not be confused with 'cocktail party chatterers', for which see **chatterbox syndrome.**)

code switching A switch between languages made by fluent bilinguals, often in the middle of a sentence.

cognitive An over-used word which has been attached to a variety of approaches which purport to describe human mental abilities. (See also **cognitive abilities; cognitive development; cognitive domains; cognitive grammar; cognitive linguistics; models.**)

cognitive abilities Human aptitudes relating to the mind, covering the capacity to perceive, learn, think and make judgements. There is considerable disagreement as to whether these abilities include language. Humans undoubtedly use general cognitive abilities when they speak in order to make sense, but the ability to handle language structure may be separate. (See also **cognitive development; innateness.**)

cognitive development The gradual unfolding of a child's ability to perceive, learn, think, and make judgements. Researchers argue about the extent to which language is based on general cognitive development, and the extent to which it depends on an independent language component within the mind, innately endowed with a knowledge of linguistic principles. (See also **innateness.**)

cognitive domains A term, found mainly in **cognitive grammar,** to describe the general areas of meaning and thought within which the human mind is naturally predisposed to operate, such as space, pain and colour. (See also **cognitive grammar.**)

cognitive grammar A type of grammar developed by Ronald Langacker which claims to be based on the way humans process language. It concerns itself with conceptual entities (things such as *book*, *grammar*) and conceptual relations (ideas such as *about*, *under*), and makes hypotheses as to how these might be interrelated.

cognitive linguistics A broad term used for any type of linguistics that purports to handle the way humans process linguistic information. It is particularly associated with the work on metaphor by George **Lakoff**.

cognitive model see **model**

cognitive psycholinguistics The study of language and mind primarily by means of logical deduction and inference, associated particularly with the work of Noam **Chomsky**. It is sometimes contrasted with **experimental psycholinguistics**, which devises experiments in order to test hypotheses about language processing. (See also **psycholinguistics**.)

cognitive science A study which covers areas of knowledge relating to the human ability to think and talk, in particular **artificial intelligence** (AI), linguistics, psychology and philosophy.

cohort model A theory of **word recognition**, which claims that hearers initially consider as possible candidates all words beginning with the same sounds as the actual word. This theory, proposed by the British psycholinguist William Marslen-Wilson, suggests that if a hearer hears [da], he or she immediately contemplates the whole army or cohort of words beginning with *da-*, such as *dance*, *dark*, *darling*, and so on, and then gradually narrows these down as it becomes clear which one is required by the linguistic structure, the meaning and the overall situation. The theory is important, in that it was one of the first to emphasise that humans consider a range of words before pinpointing the one they want, but in its early versions it possibly over-emphasised the role of word beginnings, since humans can recognise words in which they have misheard the initial sounds. (See also **speech comprehension**.)

commissures see **brain**

competence vs performance A person's linguistic system versus actual examples of language produced using the system. The distinction is important because there may be a considerable difference between someone's knowledge of their language, and what he or she is actually able to produce, as in the case of children, or people suffering from some types of speech disorder. The terms were introduced by the American linguist Noam **Chomksy** (1965), though a similar dichotomy was proposed by the Swiss linguist Ferdinand de Saussure (1915) when he spoke about *langue* vs *parole*. Recently, Chomsky has replaced competence and performance with the terms *I-language* (internalised language) vs *E-language* (externalised language).

competition model A theory of child language acquisition, which suggests that different types of 'cue' are in competition with one another in any one language. The theory, proposed by the American psycholinguist Brian Mac-Whinney, suggests that word order is a frequent and reliable 'cue' for English-speaking children, so it is initially treated by them as more important than word endings; but in a language such as German the reverse might be true. This type of theory attempts to minimise the need for an innate linguistic component in the human mind, and argues (controversially) that language is largely based on general cognitive abilities.

compound bilinguals see **bilingualism**

comprehension see **speech comprehension**

computational linguistics The general term for attempts to explore the relationhip between human language and computer systems. In practice, a large amount of work has been in the area of comprehension, and in particular **parsing** (the assignment of structure to groups of words). Various models of this process have been proposed, one of the most widespread being that known as an **ATN**. Recently, connectionist models of mental processes have become very influential. (See also **artificial intelligence; connectionism.**)

conduction aphasia A relatively uncommon type of speech disorder in which the patient is typically unable to repeat words and sentences. This disorder is rarely seen in isolation, and patients usually have other speech problems as well. A common explanation is that there has been a damage to the pathways which 'conduct' what a person hears to speech production mechanisms. These pathways possibly link areas in posterior (back) portions of the brain to others in anterior (front) portions. (See also **aphasia; brain; localisation.**)

congenital disability see **acquired disability**

connectionism An approach to mental processes which takes the connections within the human brain as inspiration. There are billions of neurons (nerve cells) in the brain, which are densely interconnected. During any brain activity, numerous brain cells are active, sending out signals to other neurons. Some signals are 'excitatory' (causing arousal), others are 'inhibitory' (causing suppression).

The result is a 'network' of interconnected units. Arousal of any units causes them to be reinforced, whereas inhibition leads to the gradual loss of a connection. Psychologists try to build computer models which simulate this connectionist viewpoint. The approach is also known as **parallel distributed processing (PDP)**, because information is thought to be processed in various different places ('distributed') at the same time ('in parallel'). There is considerable argument as to whether this type of theory is useful for dealing with language as a whole. So far, only a few areas of language have been worked on, mainly the recognition of written words by adults, and the acquisition of past tenses by children. For example, repeated hearing of a past tense ending in -d (as in *sneezed*) might recurrently excite the signals involving -d, and gradually lead to suppression of other wrongly formulated past tense forms, such as perhaps *wanten, haven*, which some children temporarily produce. Many people believe that connectionism is useful for explaining some aspects of language, particularly those which involve habit-forming, but that it cannot account for more complex aspects, such as overall judgement and planning.

connectionist models see **interactive activation model**

constraints (on language) Restrictions on what language can do, usually universal ones. For example, most, and perhaps all languages are unable to split a noun phrase such as *apples and pears*, and question only half of it. It is possible to say *Peter must buy apples and pears* and **What must Peter buy?* but not **What must Peter buy and pears?* (an asterisk denotes an impossible sentence). According to some linguists, children are pre-programmed with a knowledge of this type of constraint. (See also **innateness; minimalist program**.)

construction grammar A type of grammar, largely developed by the linguist Charles Fillmore, that assumes that the lexicon and syntax are on a continuum, rather than separate, independent components. This is particularly obvious in the case of idioms, as with the 'What's X doing Y' construction: 'What's this fly doing in my soup?', 'What's this mud doing on my carpet?', in which the syntax always contains the word *doing* and the verb *be*, and a negative can never be included (*'What's this fly not doing in my soup?' is an impossible sentence, at least in relation to the 'What's X doing Y' construction), while the meaning always involves highlighting some inconsistency or unexpected event. A grammar which links vocabulary, syntax, and meaning in this way is claimed to be more 'psychologically real' than one which tries to separate the syntax and semantics.

content vs process A controversy as to whether children naturally 'contain' pre-programmed linguistic information, or whether they are simply equipped to 'process' linguistic data efficiently. To some extent, these are two sides of the same coin, since a child who contains knowledge may be equivalent to a child who is equipped to obtain that knowledge via efficient processing. But there is a difference, since a content view commits someone to the belief that linguistic knowledge is independent of other human mental abilites, whereas a process view does not specify whether the processing principles are strictly linguistic or general cognitive ones, also used in other aspects of thinking and reasoning. (See also **innateness**.)

content word A word which has an independent meaning, such as *rose*, *king*, *jump*, as opposed to a *function word* whose task it is to relate one word to another, as 'end *of* story', 'tea *for* two'. Patients suffering from **agrammatic**

aphasia have more difficulty with function than content words, suggesting that the distinction between content and function words is a psychologically real one.

continuity vs discontinuity theories (of language origin) A controversy as to whether language developed out of animal cries in a continuous process of development, or whether it evolved alongside them. Continuity theorists suggest that animals such as the **vervet monkey** are the 'missing link' which demonstrate how animal cries came to be used as symbols, since vervets use different calls for different types of danger. Discontinuity theorists claim that babies' crying represents inherited animal calls, and that language is an extra, superimposed system, much as **birdsong** has been superimposed on a simple set of calls. (See also **crying**.)

contrast, principle of see **uniqueness principle**

conversational implicature see **co-operative principle**

convolution see **brain**

cooing The 'goo-goo' type sounds produced by babies from around six weeks onwards. The sounds are superficially vowel-like, and are fairly unlike any 'real' speech sounds, which first appear during the subsequent **babbling** stage. (See also **child language**.)

co-operative principle A guideline which human beings follow when they communicate, which states that they behave in a helpful way to each other, according to the American philosopher Paul Grice (1967). The principle is broken down into four sub-sections or 'maxims': the maxim of 'quantity' (give the right amount of information), the maxim of 'quality' (be truthful), the maxim of 'relevance' (talk to the point), the maxim of 'manner' (be clear and orderly). If a speaker breaks these maxims, the hearer assumes that the co-operative principle is still in operation, and that the speaker has broken a maxim intentionally, in order to convey some message. For example, if someone said: *Peter is a dinosaur* which is blatantly untrue and so breaks the maxim of quality, the hearer would assume that the speaker did this on purpose, and would therefore make inferences about Peter's behaviour, perhaps that he is out of date. The breaking of maxims in order to imply unspoken information is known as *conversational implicature*. It forms an important part of how humans interpret each other's speech and writing. The co-operative principle is somewhat overgeneral, and attempts have been made to make it more precise, and also to supplement it with principles of politeness, which sometimes override the simple notion of co-operation. (See also **interpretation; speech act theory; speech comprehension**.)

co-ordinate bilinguals see **bilingualism**

corpus callosum see **brain**

correction see **negative evidence**

correspondence hypothesis A suggestion made in the early 1960s that the way in which humans produce sentences corresponded with the way in which a **transformational grammar** described their formation. Comprehension was assumed to work in reverse. This was soon realised to be unrealistic. It was superseded by the **Derivational Theory of Complexity**, which linked human processing more weakly to a transformational grammar – though it in turn has now been abandoned. Recent work has shown speech processing to be considerably more complex than was once assumed. (See also **speech comprehension; speech production**.)

cortex see **brain**

creativity The human ability to produce and understand an indefinite number of new sentences which they may have never heard before, also known as *open-endedness* or *productivity*. If someone heard the question *Do kangaroos lay eggs?*, he or she would be able to comprehend the question, and answer appropriately, even though this sentence might never have been uttered before. Creativity is also used to describe the human ability to respond freely: on hearing a particular utterance, humans do not have to make a fixed response. If someone asked: *What's the time?*, they could either give the time, or say *Buy yourself a watch*, or *I haven't a clue*, or anything else they wished. True creativity is thought to be absent from most, perhaps all natural animal communication systems. Apes such as **Washoe**, who have been taught sign language show a limited creativity, in that they can sometimes combine signs in a novel way. (See **animal communication; ape signing**.)

critical period A crucial time within a child's life during which he or she must be exposed to language, according to Eric Lenneberg, who first proposed the notion (1967). Lenneberg argued that the critical period began at the age of around two, and lasted till adolescence, after which language could not be properly acquired. The notion of rigid critical period has been disputed. Language learning may be in progress from birth, and there is no evidence for an absolute cut-off point at adolescence. Most researchers agree that young brains are more adaptable and supple than older ones, and suggest that there is a **sensitive period,** in which language learning ability tails off gradually. (See also **child language.**)

crying The shouts and sobs of human babies. Different types of cries can be identified (anger, hunger, pain, and so on) which are recognisable world-wide. This has led to claims that crying is comparable to the inherited communication system of many animals, a view adopted by those who believe in a *discontinuity theory* of language origin. They argue that crying exists alongside language, much as birdcalls exist alongside birdsong. Crying strengthens the lungs and exercises the vocal cords, so helping to prepare the infant for language. But the large amount of apparently pointless crying indulged in by some infants indicates that it may originally have had a subsidiary survival purpose, as a reminder to parents that their offspring exist. Deafened ringdoves apparently forget about their nestlings, and lay more eggs. (See also **birdsong; continuity vs discontinuity theories.**)

D

DAT (dementia of Alzheimer's type) A mental disorder characterised by extreme forgetfulness, and in its later stages, loss of language. It is referred to as SDAT (senile dementia of Alzheimer's type) if the patient is elderly. It was first clearly documented by a German, Alois Alzheimer, when in 1901 a fifty-one-year-old woman suffering from severe memory problems was admitted to the psychiatric hospital in Frankfurt where he worked. Most subsequent studies of the language problems of DAT patients have concentrated on the vocabulary, since severe word-finding problems are a noticeable feature. A patient's syntax is also affected, though some overlearned phrases often remain, such as 'Hello, how are you today?'. As the disease progresses, patients become progressively less capable of understanding or producing language. (See also **automatic speech**.)

deafness see **Ildefonso; Kelli; Nicaraguan signing community**

deception see **lying**

decoding Understanding speech. The metaphor comes from communication theory, in which messages are 'decoded' (deciphered) or 'encoded' (put into a code ready to be sent). (See also **speech comprehension**.)

deep dyslexia see **dyslexia**

deep structure see **transformational grammar**

deep structure ambiguity see **ambiguity**

delphinology The study of dolphins. At one time, it was claimed that the elaborate communication system of dolphins might be similar to human language in its ability to handle novel topics. Two dolphins (Buzz and Doris) were thought to be communicating creatively with one another, by explaining which lever to pull in order to obtain fish. Later, it emerged that they had simply devised memory tricks which involved sounds. Dolphins can communicate more accurately and more effectively than humans about shapes of objects, but they do not appear to be able to handle novel topics, a crucial property of human language (**creativity**). (See also **animal communication**.)

derailment The mistaken production of a word which has the same beginning as the intended one. For example, *The motorway* (motorcade) *passed close by me*. The speaker appears to have been 'derailed' from his or her original intention, and uttered a word which may be more frequently used than the intended one. This is one kind of **selection error**, a mistake made in the choice of a vocabulary item. It forms part of a larger category of **slips of the tongue** (speech errors) which provide important information about how speakers find the words they want (**word retrieval**) when they produce speech. (See also **speech production**.)

Derivational Theory of Complexity (DTC) A theory briefly popular in the 1960s which proposed that, when a person comprehended a sentence, its relative difficulty could be correlated with the level of complexity predicted in a **transformational grammar** for forming or deriving that sentence. Easy-to-understand sentences were assumed to have very few transformations, and difficult ones were thought to have many. It turned out that there was very little correlation between difficulty of comprehension and transformational complexity. Other more sophisticated models of comprehension have now replaced DTC. (See also **parsing; speech comprehension**.)

design features (of language) Basic characteristics of human language which the American linguist Charles Hockett attempted to identify in the late 1950s and early 1960s. They included **creativity**, **displacement** and **structure-dependence**, features now thought to be either rare or non-existent in **animal communication**.

developmental disability see **acquired disability**

developmental dyslexia see **acquired disability; dyslexia**

developmental psycholinguistics The study of child language. (See **child language**.)

dichotic listening An experimental technique in which a person is asked to wear headphones, and is then played a different sound or word into each ear. It was originally used by neurologists to discover which side of the brain is primarily used to process language: words played into the right ear are processed by the left side of the brain (and vice versa), so if a person paid more attention to the words played into the right ear, then this would show he or she was processing speech primarily in the left hemisphere, as is the norm. The technique can also be used to show that a person can process words without being aware of it: if an ambiguous word such as *put out* is played into the right ear, it is unclear whether this means 'extinguish' or 'display'. But if the word *extinguish* or *display* is simultaneously played into the left ear, then the hearer usually gives the meaning of *put out* which fits the word played into the unattended ear, even though he or she is unable to explain how this conclusion was reached. (See also **cerebral dominance; lateralisation; localisation; word recognition**.)

discontinuity theory see **continuity vs discontinuity theories**

displacement The ability to communicate about matters which are removed in time and place. This is one way in which human language differs from most animal communication systems, though **bee dancing** involves some displacement. Displacement is related to the more important property of **creativity**, the ability to communicate about novel topics.

dolphins see **delphinology**

double articulation see **duality**

DTC see **Derivational Theory of Complexity**

duality also known as *double articulation* The 'double-layer-ing' of human language. Each sound is mostly mean-ingless by itself, but acquires meaning when combined with others.

dys- A prefix meaning 'difficulty with'. It is used to describe a variety of language disorders, as in **dyslexia** 'difficulty with reading'. It is sometimes used interchangeably with the prefix *a-* meaning literally 'without', as in *alexia* literally 'without reading ability'. (See also **a-/an-**.)

dysarthria see **a-/an-**; **anarthria**

dysgraphia Literally 'difficulty with writing'. The term is applied to a wide range of writing disorders, and is often used interchangeably with the word *agraphia* 'without writing ability'. (See also **a-/an-**; **dys-**.)

dyslexia Literally 'difficulty with reading'. The term is applied to a variety of reading disorders, which may be caused by injury (*acquired dyslexia*), or may be of unknown origin (*developmental dyslexia*). Some types of dyslexia are due to problems with vision, while others are due to language problems. Dyslexia can be broadly divided into *surface dyslexia*, in which the reading errors are similar in sound to the original, as in *beggar* for 'begin', and *deep dyslexia*, where the reading errors are similar in meaning to the original, as in *fire* for 'heat'. The latter type indicates serious damage to pathways within the brain. Occasionally, the term *alexia* 'without reading ability' is used interchangeably with dyslexia. (See also **a-/an-**.)

dysphasia see **aphasia**

| E |

echolalia Exact repetition, as if by an echo. In some speech disorders, patients are unable to respond spontaneously, but simply repeat back what is said to them.

E-language see **competence vs performance**

EEG see **electroencephalogram**

electroencephalogram (EEG) A recording of the electrical activity within the brain, made by placing electrodes on the head.

emergence vs acquisition see **acquisition (of language)**

encoding Producing speech. A metaphor from communication theory, in which messages are 'encoded' (put into code and sent) or 'decoded' (deciphered). (See also **speech production**.)

epigenesis vs preformation Development via gradual growth and reorganisation, versus the idea that an animal's characteristic features have always been present.

ERPs see **event-related potentials**

error data see **slip of the ear; slip of the eye; slip of the hand; slip of the pen; slip of the tongue**

event-related potentials Electrical activity within the brain which can be measured and correlated with an external 'event' such as presenting the subject with a particular stimulus.

exchange error An error in which a sound, syllable, word or sign changes place with another, in speaking, writing, or signing. For example: *lowing the morn* (mowing the lawn), *cuss and kiddle* (kiss and cuddle), *nouvelais beaujeau* (Beaujolais nouveau), *sleep in my talk* (talk in my sleep). Such errors are also known as *transpositions* or *metatheses*. Sound exchanges at the beginning of words are sometimes called **spoonerisms**, after the Reverend A. Spooner (1844–1930) who is reputed to have made errors of this type. Such **slips of the tongue** (speech errors) provide important information about speech production. Exchange errors are **assemblage errors**, in that items which have been correctly selected are then wrongly assembled. They show that speech is not planned word by word, but in larger chunks, since items must have been chosen prior to being assembled in order. **Slips of the pen** and **slips of the hand** provide similar information about writing and signing.

expansions An enlarged version of a child's utterance. For example, if a child says: *kitty milk*, an adult is likely to enlarge this to *Yes, kitty is drinking her milk*. At one time, expansions were thought to be of major importance in child language acquisition, but further research suggested that continuing the conversation and recasting the sentence may be more helpful, as when an adult says, *Kitty's thirsty! Shall we give her some more milk?* Such observations show that children cannot be taught language like parrots, they work it out for themselves, and progress at their own speed. (See also **caregiver language**.)

experimental paradox The 'no-win' situation in which those conducting psycholinguistic experiments often find themselves: the more perfect the experiment, the less like real life it is, and the more likely it is that those being tested may be giving unnatural responses. However, the more like real life the experiment, the less possible it is to control external factors which are likely to affect it. (See also **experimental psycholinguistics**.)

experimental psycholinguistics The study of language and mind by means of carefully devised experiments. A perfect experiment is almost impossible, because rigid experimental conditions destroy the naturalness of the situation, a dilemma known as the **experimental paradox**. However, a number of well-used techniques, such as **lexical decision tasks** and **phoneme monitoring** have proved valuable in discovering more about speech processing. Experimental psycholinguists are often contrasted with **cognitive psycholinguists**, who mostly propose theories about the mind on the basis of logical reasoning and inference.

expressive vs receptive aphasia Speech disorders involving primarily speech production versus those involving primarily speech comprehension. (See also **aphasia**.)

F

family resemblance phenomenon The situation in which no one definition can cover all the meanings of a word, because the various meanings are like the members of a family which each possess some family characteristics, but no one family member possesses them all. The philosopher Ludwig Wittgenstein (1953) named the phenomenon, pointing out problems with the word *game*. Each type of game shares some characteristics with some other game, but no one definition can cover all games. The family resemblance problem is partially solved by suggesting that humans understand meaning by selecting a **prototype**, or typical example. (See also **prototype theory**.)

felicity conditions see **speech act theory**

feral children Also known as 'wild children'. Children raised by animals, or away from human contact. A famous case is the eighteenth-century French boy, Victor of Aveyron, who, after being found, eventually died without language, and may have been mentally handicapped, perhaps due to his early poor diet. A recent, carefully studied example of someone deprived of early human contact is **Genie**.

filled pause A pause in speech filled by *er-er* or *um-um* or similar. (See also **pause**.)

fine-tuning hypothesis The suggestion that caregivers (those in charge of children) automatically adjust their level of syntax (grammatical structure) to that of their children. In fact, this does not happen. Instead, caregivers adjust their speech to their children's interests. This suggests that children rely to a large extent on their own internal mechanisms for extracting language. They are not just being 'taught' by their parents. (See also **caregiver language**.)

finger spelling see **sign language**

'fis' phenomenon The ability of children to recognise that their own 'mangled' words are incorrect. The phenomenon was named when a small boy referred to his inflated plastic fish as a *fis*. The observer asked: *This is your fis?* (imitating the child's pronunciation). *No*, said the child, *my fis*. He continued to reject the *fis* pronunciation. Finally, the observer said: *That is your fish?* (with adult pronunciation). *Yes*, replied the child, *my fis*. Such anecdotes indicate that children have a more accurate mental representation of words than they themselves are able to produce. Yet production alone is not always the problem, since children often use a required sound in other words. A possible explanation of the 'fis' phenomenon is that children have not yet discovered which tongue and lip movements are linked with each sound.

fluent aphasia A speech disorder in which the patient produces a fluent flow of words, though these often do not make sense, and may include 'jargon' or nonsense words. For example, *My father, he's the biggest envelope that ever worked in Ipswich*; *There was the one of indicate of vintry of foxing with one sort of matters from one orders*. Such patients usually have serious comprehension difficulties. The disorder is typically associated with damage to posterior (back) portions of the brain, especially around **Wernicke's Area**. Alternative names for the problem are *Wernicke's aphasia*, and, when nonsense words predominate, *jargon aphasia*. The symptoms are sometimes described as displaying *paragrammatism*, meaning 'deviant grammar', in contrast to **agrammatism** 'absent grammar'. (See also **agrammatic aphasia; aphasia**.)

fMRI see **functional magnetic resonance imaging**

frame A mental plan of an area of knowledge. The term was proposed by the philosopher Marvin Minsky, who suggested that people have 'remembered frameworks' (1975), which enable them to handle the world. For example, if someone mentioned a *bath*, the average English person would mentally activate a bathroom frame, which would have certain predictable features, such as a bath with bath taps, a shower, and a wash-basin. Any bathroom features mentioned would be slotted into this stored frame, so making sense of sentences, such as: *Penelope's just bought bath taps shaped like dolphins.* The notion of frame overlaps with that of a **script**, which is a stored memory of a typical sequence of events. The setting up of frames and scripts is one possible way in which humans interpret the speech they hear. (See also **interpretation; speech comprehension.**)

freezes Pairs of words which have been apparently 'frozen' in a fixed order, such as *bread and butter, husband and wife, knife and fork.* Such sequences show how sensitive humans are to *collocations*, words which are routinely found together.

frequency effect The phenomenon that frequently occurring words are recognised more quickly than less common ones. This apparently obvious observation is not very easy to interpret. Some researchers have suggested that less common words are (metaphorically) more faintly inked in in people's minds. Others have proposed that the phenomenon is due to humans searching for words by going through those stored one after the other, starting with the commonly used ones. (See also **word recognition.**)

Freudian slips Speech errors which are either partly or wholly caused by some disturbing influence outside the intended utterance, as in 'You haven't written a *bread* (book)', said by someone who who was leafing through a cookery book. According to the Austrian psychologist Sigmund Freud (1901), such errors were often due to intrusive thoughts about sex or other private matters, as in when a woman said *Hose* (knickers) instead of *Haus(e)* (house), after she had omitted mention of *Hose* when talking about items of clothing which got drenched with perspiration on walking holidays. In fact, **slips of the tongue** (speech errors) only occasionally reveal a person's suppressed thoughts, and more usually provide straightforward information about speech production. (See also **speech production.**)

functional magnetic resonance imaging (fMRI) A brain-imaging procedure, which shows changes in blood flow depending on the task a patient is being asked to carry out. The more complex the task, the greater the blood flow. This technique enables researchers to distinguish between blood-flow patterns in simple linguistic tasks, such as straight repetition, and more complex ones, such as attaching appropriate verbs to nouns, as with *hit* to 'hammer'. This procedure has shown differences between *intransitive verbs* (verbs without an object, as in *she jumped*), and *transitive verbs* (verbs with an object, as in *he chased the mouse*). This neurological evidence backs up a long-standing linguistic viewpoint.

G

gap-filling A gap-filling model of comprehension suggests that if, on hearing a sentence, a listener cannot immediately find a structural slot for an item, he or she holds it in memory until a 'gap' appears, into which the item can be placed. For example, in a sentence beginning *Which book*, the phrase *which book* would be held in memory until an 'unfilled gap' appeared, perhaps *Which book did Henry buy [ ]?*. The 'gap' is after *buy* since the verb *buy* normally requires an object.

garden-path sentences Sentences in which listeners are initially led astray, 'up the garden path', as they try to interpret them, as in the sentence: *Concorde flies like a bird: they burrow under its feathers*. Hearers initially interpret this as a statement about a Concorde aeroplane. But they have been led 'up the garden path', because the second part shows that it must be interpreted as 'There is a kind of fly, called a concorde fly, which has a liking for birds'. These misinterpretations can sometimes provide valuable information about the processes of **speech comprehension**.

gating An experimental technique in which a researcher allows a small amount of a word to be heard, then cuts off the rest with a 'gate'. Progressively larger portions of two similar words, such as *spook*, *spoon*, might be played, until a recognition point is reached. Gating shows that people routinely recognise a word before the speaker has finished saying it.

Genie A deeply deprived American girl, who did not begin acquiring language until she was almost 14. Genie was kept in near isolation and forbidden to utter sounds by a father who was probably mentally ill. When rescued in 1970, and exposed to language, she began to acquire it at a much slower rate than younger children, and has never learned to speak normally. It is unclear whether her problems are due to physical damage, emotional disturbance, or late exposure to language. Some people have argued that her difficulties provide evidence for a **critical period** for language acquisition, a time set aside by nature for language development, which Genie is presumed to have missed.

gestures Movements of the body or limbs for communication. Such movements may accompany speech. They are not to be confused with **sign language**.

government and binding theory see **Chomsky**

GPC rules see **grapheme–phoneme correspondence rules**

grammar The linguistic system of a language. The term 'grammar' is commonly used for the whole system, comprising *phonology* (sound patterns), *syntax* (word structure and word arrangements), and *semantics* (meaning patterns). It is often used interchangeably to mean both a person's internalised grammar, and a linguist's attempt to describe this, which do not necessarily correspond. The question of whether a linguist's formulation is a reliable representation of a person's internal system is often referred to as the **psychological reality problem**. According to some linguists, a certain amount of the human grammatical system is genetically inbuilt, and this innate component is referred to as **Universal Grammar (UG)**.

grapheme–phoneme correspondence rules Principles for converting written letters into spoken sounds, which are presumed to be known by anyone who can read. There is some argument as to how much conversion is involved in reading, since some fast readers may by-pass the process in silent reading. However, slow readers may always carry out this conversion, and it is also essential in reading aloud.

grey matter see **brain**

grey parrot see **Alex**

grooming talking A name sometimes given to *phatic communion* or 'talking for the sake of talking'. The name comes from the claim that humans 'groom' each other mostly with words, rather than with the tactile methods used by other apes. According to one theory, grooming talking developed when humans started to live in large groups, and so did not have enough time to groom everybody else manually.

guided learning The notion that inbuilt biological factors guide humans and animals in certain directions as they learn. This viewpoint is replacing the old **nature vs nurture controversy**, which assumed that instinct and learning are opposites. Animals were once thought to behave mostly by instinct, and humans by learning. But instinctual behaviour may form a large component of learning. For example, bees do not know in advance about every type of flower: they have an instinctive preference for certain colours, scents and shapes, but they have to learn how these are arranged in the flowers in their own environment. Similarly, learned behaviour may involve instinct. Humans, when they learn to drive a car, use instinctive behaviour when they judge distances, or co-ordinate eye and hand movements. The relationship between instinct and learning is therefore considerably more complex than was once assumed. Human language is now thought by many to involve guided learning. (See also **innateness**.)

guppy effect Also known as the 'pet fish' problem, since a guppy is a type of fish commonly kept in household aquariums. Humans understand the world partly by setting up **prototypes** which encapsulate **mental models** of the world around. English speakers might have a notion of a protoypical 'pet' as something playful and cuddly, and of a prototypical 'fish' as something slimy and fast-swimming. The problem is how they combine these two, to form a new model 'pet fish'. An important conclusion is that the human mind does not work from a fixed set of images, but is always actively adjusting its mental models to fit in with new information.

H

handedness Hand preference. Most humans are right-handed, and this usually correlates with the location of speech in the left hemisphere of the **brain**. The brain's left hemisphere controls the right side of the human body. The situation with left-handed humans is not so clear-cut. Most of them have speech located in the left hemisphere, but in others it is found in the right hemisphere – and in others in both hemispheres.

hard-wired vs soft-wired A way of referring to the **nature vs nurture controversy**

Harvard children Adam, Eve and Sarah, three American children studied extensively by Roger Brown and his associates at Harvard University in the 1960s. (See also **child language**.)

HAS see **high amplitude sucking**

heredity The relationship between heredity and language is not well understood. Several families have been found, some of whose members have difficulty in adding endings onto words, and in using pronouns. They appear able to learn whole words, but cannot alter their form, or put in pronouns as substitutes. Certain language problems such as **dyslexia** tend to recur within family groups. But it would be misleading to talk about a language 'gene', since sufferers of language disorders often have disabilities which go beyond language, and several genes may be involved in any language disorder.

hesitation pauses see **pause**

high amplitude sucking (HAS) The energy with which babies suck has been shown to correlate with their interest level. Infants who heard a repeated sound gradually lost interest, but when this sound was changed to a different one, they recommenced strong sucking. This experiment showed that children as young as four months can hear the difference between B and P. According to some researchers, infants as young as four days old react with strong sucking when played their own language, but they remain unreceptive to a non-native language. This suggests that infants may have become acclimatised to the rhythms of their own language before birth, when in the womb.

holophrase A single word which represents a whole phrase or sentence in early child language, as in *No* meaning 'I don't want to go to bed', *Nana* 'I want a banana', *Mine* 'That's my shoe'. There is considerable disagreement as to the interpretation of such utterances, though almost all researchers agree that children mostly intend to communicate more than they are capable of expressing.

horse-race approach (to word recognition) A claim that when a hearer tries to recognise a spoken word, he or she normally considers several possible candidate words simultaneously, as if the words were horses competing against one another in a race. This **parallel processing** approach is now considered more likely than a **serial processing** method, in which the hearer checks out one possibility at a time.

I

ICMs see **idealised cognitive models**

idealised cognitive models (ICMs) The mental models of a person's world which he or she builds up in order to cope with life. They are partly private, partly shared with other speakers, and are also sometimes known as **cognitive domains, frames** or **scripts**. They are reflected in a person's and a nation's speech and writing, though extend more widely, beyond the realm of language.

idiom A phrase which cannot be interpreted by amalgamating the meaning of the individual words, but must be learned as a whole, as in *kick the bucket* 'die'. The extent to which idioms can be manipulated varies. *The bucket was kicked* is unacceptable, but *We pulled his leg* 'we teased him' and *His leg was pulled* are equally possible. Idioms are very numerous, and the extent to which they can be manipulated may shed considerable light on the way humans handle language.

I-language see **competence vs performance**

Ildefonso A deaf Mexican who was almost thirty before he learned sign and written language. He did not at first possess the **naming insight,** the realisation that words can be 'names' for things, but acquired this in stages: first, he learned names for numbers; second, names for people and things; third, names for actions.

imageability The extent to which something can be visualised. So-called **basic level categories,** such as *dog, chair,* have strong imageability, since images of them can readily be formed in the mind.

image schemata Mental diagrams that recur among humans, some of which may be innate (inborn). For example, an idea that 'up is good, down is bad' is widespread, as in 'go up in the world', 'be down in the dumps'. Exceptions can be found: high is not usually good if meat is involved, but strong image schema similarities are found around the world.

imitation Accurate copying. The possible role of imitation in child language has been much discussed. Children do not just imitate their caregivers when they acquire language, as is clear from utterances such as *Mummy comed*, *Me taked a bissy*, which could not have been copied from an adult. 'Imitation and reduction' is a feature of child language, when children imitate and shorten an adult utterance, as in *Doggie walk* in response to an adult's: 'Let's take the doggie for a walk', though such imitation does not obviously improve their language skills. 'Imitation and expansion' is a feature of adult speech to children, in which adults imitate and expand a child's utterance, as in *Yes, pussy's drinking her milk* in response to a child's: *Pussy milk*. This may benefit a learner, if the expansion fits in with an area of language which the child is working on at the time. At one time, caregiver speech was underrated as a source of child learning. But the extent to which a child pays attention to caregiver speech and tries to copy it may vary from child to child. (See also **caregiver speech; expansions**.)

implicational 'rule' 'If a language has X, it will also have Y'. For example, 'if a language has its object after the verb, as in *climb the hill*, then it is likely to have prepositions as in *up the hill*'. Such implicational 'rules' are more usually strong propensities than absolute rules. They seem to be a type of *analogy* – the tendency in language for things that are similar in meaning to become similar in form – and may be the basis of the claim by Chomsky that children **set parameters** when they learn to speak.

implicature see **co-operative principle**

innately guided learning see **guided learning**

innateness (of language) The property of being genetically inbuilt. It does not mean that language actually 'exists' at birth, merely that it is pre-programmed to develop as the individual matures (**maturationally controlled behaviour**). All researchers agree that something about language must be innate, otherwise the family cat would acquire speech. The crucial question therefore is the extent to which the human ability to speak is a separate component (module) within the mind, prewired along fixed lines, and to what extent language is the outcome of the human capacity for thinking (general cognitive abilities). The American linguist Noam **Chomsky** has argued strongly in favour of innateness, though his views have changed considerably over the last half-century. His earlier proposals for a **Language Acquisition Device** (1965) have been replaced by claims that children are pre-programmed with an outline knowledge of **Universal Grammar (UG)** (1986, 1995, 2002). (See also **modularity**.)

input vs uptake A distinction between the speech which a child hears spoken (the input) and the utterances he or she pays attention to (the uptake). In general, children's uptake fits in with their own level of understanding, and not necessarily with the output of the surrounding speakers (See also **caregiver language**.)

intelligence see **cognitive abilities**

interactive activation model A model of word recognition and word retrieval (word finding) which suggests that any word or part of a word automatically activates other similar words, and that – metaphorically – electric current is passing to and fro between these aroused words. For example, the word *sparrow* might activate other similar-sounding words such as *spanner* and *spatter*, and also other bird-names such as *blackbird*, *thrush*, *swallow*. Each of these would in turn activate further words. Those in which the meaning and the sound were similar to the **target** (word being sought) would become particularly aroused, as perhaps in the case of *sparrow* and *swallow*, and would stay in a high state of excitation. Gradually, other words would fade away. Eventually, only the required word would remain. The activation is not just moving outwards to more words, as in a closely related *spreading activation model*, but is moving backwards and forwards between the activated words, and pieces of word. Such a model overlaps with *connectionist models*. (See also **connectionism; word recognition; word retrieval.**)

interpretation The assignment of meaning to a spoken utterance or written sentence. This is one of several overlapping processes involved in **speech comprehension,** the others being **speech perception** (identification of sounds), **word recognition,** and **parsing** (assignment of structure to words recognised). Part of the interpretation comes directly out of the words and structures used. If someone said: *The donkey kicked the rabbit,* it is clear that one kind of animal struck another kind of animal with its foot or hoof. But in real life, the literal interpretation is often only indirectly related to the speaker's intention: a woman who says *I'm tired* is superficially conveying the information that she is weary, but she may primarily be trying to communicate some other message, such as: 'Can we go home now?', or 'Please stop talking'. It is difficult to know which of the numerous possible messages is being conveyed, and various proposals have been put forward for how hearers come to a decision over this. A widespread view is that a principle of communication known as the **co-operative principle** is an important part of this process. Others have proposed an overlapping view, involving **speech act theory**. A further problem is how humans understand one another, when conversation often assumes considerable mutual knowledge which is not explicitly mentioned. One suggestion is that humans are working with **frames**, remembered frameworks into which they slot the matters being talked about, and **scripts**, typical sequences of events.

J

Jakobson, R. O. (1896–1982) Russian linguist, later a naturalised American, whose wide-ranging interests had considerable influence on various areas within linguistics, including child language and aphasia. Roman (Osipovič) Jakobson claimed that children develop the sounds of their language in a fixed, universal order, and also that aphasics (sufferers from speech disorders) lose these sounds in the reverse order to that in which children acquired them (the **regression hypothesis**). These ideas have turned out to be largely unfounded, and their value is primarily in the research which they inspired. (See also **aphasia**.)

jargon aphasia see **fluent aphasia**

K

Kanzi The name of a male bonobo or pygmy chimp who has learned to communicate with his human trainers by manipulating symbols on a keyboard. He is able to combine symbols, and, according to his trainers, has invented some 'rules' – combinations of symbols which always occur in a particular order. He is also able to comprehend some spoken language, and to respond appropriately to commands, such as obeying a novel request to throw a ball in a river. (See also **ape signing, Lana.**)

Kelli A blind child who learned to speak without any apparent difficulty, in spite of her visual handicap. She is able to discuss her blindness coherently: 'You guys see with your eyes . . . I see with my hands.' She learned to speak by paying particular attention to words which occur together, and was able, for example, to reliably distinguish between the words *look* and *see* by noticing that they behaved differently in the sentences they occurred in, as 'You look like a kangaroo', 'Come and see the kitty.'

knowing how vs knowing that A distinction between knowing *how* to do something, such as riding a bicycle (sometimes called *procedural knowledge*), and knowing *that* something is so, such as knowing that a bicycle is a two-wheeled method of transport (sometimes called *declarative knowledge*). Humans know *how* to speak, but in addition, gradually build up knowledge and beliefs about language.

Koko The name of a female lowland gorilla who was taught a simplified form of **American Sign Language**. Koko, like the signing chimps **Washoe** and **Nim Chimpsky**, acquired over one hundred signs, and learned to combine these. Koko showed that apes are not the only animals who can acquire signs. A problem with all these animals is that they tend to be highly active, and also sometimes sign with both hands simultaneously, so it is sometimes hard to interpret the messages sent.

L

LAD see **Language Acquisition Device**

Lakoff, George A linguist from the University of California at Berkeley, whose work, and particularly his book *Women, Fire and Dangerous Things* (1987) were important in the foundation of **cognitive linguistics.**

Lana The name of a female chimp who was trained to communicate by pressing computer keys, each of which has an abstract design representing a word. Beginning in 1971, her progress was monitored by Duane Rumbaugh and Sue Savage-Rumbaugh, at the Yerkes Regional Primate Research Centre in Atlanta, Georgia. Like other apes, such as **Washoe,** she was able to handle arbitrary symbols, and to combine them creatively to some extent, as in the phrase BANANA WHICH-IS GREEN for 'cucumber'. Unlike the signing apes, she kept to a strict word order (as she had been trained). However, her 'speech' shows little sign of structure, so her communication system is unlike human language, in that it is probably not structure dependent. Such ape studies are useful in that they show how much of human language is likely to be linked to general cognitive abilities, and how much might be genetically programmed. (See also **ape signing; structure dependence.**)

Language Acquisition Device (LAD) A system for learning language with which every human is innately endowed, according to the American linguist Noam **Chomsky,** in his influential book *Aspects of the theory of syntax* (1965). LAD had three major components: (1) knowledge of linguistic universals, which included information about the basic building blocks of language, and some general principles of language organisation; (2) a hypothesis-making device, to enable children to make increasingly complex guesses or hypotheses about the rules underlying the speech they heard around them; and (3) an evaluation measure, so that children could decide which grammar was best, in case they came up with more than one possibility. It proved impossible to specify the actual workings of such a device, with the evaluation measure causing particular difficulty. In more recent writings, Chomsky has put forward an alternative view of language acquisition, which proposes that children supplement fixed principles of **Universal Grammar** with a series of forced choices between various pre-ordained options. This is known as a **parameter-setting** model.

langue see **competence vs performance**

LARSP (Language Assessment, Remediation and Screening Procedure) A language assessment procedure used by clinical linguists, devised by British linguists D. Crystal, P. Fletcher and M. Garman (1976). It was the first diagnostic screening to make use of linguistic principles, and therefore potentially enabled a reliable overall picture to be obtained of a child's or patient's linguistic capabilities. Several other similar procedures are now available, and their importance is that they can check whether children can produce the type of speech that might be expected of them at a given age.

late closure (principle of) A proposed **speech comprehension** strategy: 'Do not close off phrases prematurely, keep them open as long as possible'; in other words 'Try to include each new item within the phrase currently being processed'. For example, in the sentence *Louise realised at midnight the house had been burgled*, the phrase *at midnight* could be associated with either *realised* or *the house had been burgled*. Late closure predicts that hearers will be likely to link it with *realised*, since the phrase containing this verb has been left open, waiting for possible extra additions. The role of **perceptual strategies** (rule-of-thumb procedures) in **parsing** (assignment of structure to groups of words in comprehension) is still unclear, since they interact with lexical (vocabulary) knowledge in a way not yet fully understood.

lateralisation The location of an aspect of human behaviour in one hemisphere (half) of the brain. Language is usually controlled by the left hemisphere, which is the dominant one in the majority of humans. According to Eric Lenneberg, in his influential book *Biological foundations of language* (1967), lateralisation of language is a gradual event, which occurs between the ages of two and thirteen. However, recent research suggests that this is unlikely. The left hemisphere may be specialised for language from birth: experiments with infants only a few weeks old indicate that they process speech sounds with the left hemisphere (the direction of their gaze indicates which hemisphere they are primarily using). Lenneberg claimed that the supposed lateralisation period was a **critical period** for language acquisition, a view that now seems unlikely. (See also **cerebral dominance**.)

Laura (child) see **chatterbox syndrome, Marta**

layering see **polysemy**

learnability problem The puzzle of how children learn language, when (according to a number of researchers) they do not receive sufficient information from the language they are exposed to to do this. Consequently (it is argued), they must be innately pre-programmed for language in some detail. This viewpoint is particularly associated with the American linguist Noam **Chomsky**, who has put forward a number of proposals for innate mechanisms. In 1965 he argued that children have an inbuilt **Language Acquisition Device**. More recently, he has altered his views, and proposed that children are pre-programmed with a knowledge of **Universal Grammar**, which includes information about certain options available to human languages. Children have to decide which one to select in a process known as **parameter setting**.

left hemisphere see **brain**

left-to-right processing An approach to sentence comprehension which suggests that listeners work in an orderly way from the beginning of a sentence to the end. This approach is appealing, because it can be simulated on a computer, as in the left-to-right model known as an **ATN**. This view of **parsing** (the assignment of structure to groups of words) contrasts with a **perceptual strategy** viewpoint, which proposes that hearers jump to conclusions on the basis of outline clues. (See also **speech comprehension**.)

lemma A hypothetical abstract mental representation of a word, the equivalent of a *headword* in a dictionary, which is the form given before all the variant forms are listed: in a dictionary entry, the headword *talk* appears before forms such as *talked*, *talking* and so on. Psycholinguists argue as to whether a lemma has true psychological reality. An alternative viewpoint is that all forms of a word are linked in a network, with no abstract representation required.

Lenneberg, Eric (1921–1975) A pioneering psycholinguist, whose book *The biological basis of language* (1967) initiated a new era in the understanding of **maturationally controlled behaviour.**

lexical access An early stage of word recognition, in which sounds are matched against probable words. An unsolved question is the form in which the sounds are matched. Some researchers argue that acoustic signals (unstructured sounds) are fitted directly onto possible words, though most assume that acoustic signals are first organised into either phonemes (sound units) or syllables. One possibility is that the method used depends on the language involved. The overall process of **word recognition** is a complex one. Many people now assume that it consists of a narrowing down of the multiple possibilities which become available at the lexical access stage. (See also **speech perception.**)

lexical ambiguity see **ambiguity**

lexical decision task A technique used in experimental studies, in which people are asked to decide as quickly as possible whether a sequence of sounds or letters, such as *grank*, *find*, *vilk*, is a word or not. In its simplest form, this procedure can provide information about the speed of word recognition. It is often combined with other tasks, in order to provide more detailed information. For example, a researcher might see if recognition of a real word could be speeded up by presenting a word with a similar meaning just before it. All studies indicate that words are recognised in a fraction of a second (one sixth of a second, according to one study), and often before the whole word has been heard. (See also **word recognition**.)

lexical diffusion The gradual spreading of a change across all similar words in the lexicon. In the twentieth century, a group of scholars known as the 'Neogrammarians' claimed that sound changes happened simultaneously, and with no exceptions, if the changing sound was in a similar place in the word. Now it is realised that changes creep across at a fairly similar time, but not simultaneously. So someone who says *bu'er* (*butter*) might not necessarily say *gu'er* (*gutter*) or *stu'er* (*stutter*), even though in a few decades these words probably will be pronounced in the same way, and future generations might get the superficial impression that the changes happened at the same time. From the point of view of psycholinguistics, the interest of lexical diffusion is that children, when they acquire phonological and morphological 'rules', display a similar spreading across the vocabulary as happens in change.

lexical priming see **priming**

lexicon see **mental lexicon**

limited scope formula A pattern restricted to a small area of language. Such patterns are used by young children for producing utterances when they are at the **two-word stage**, according to the American psychologist Martin Braine (1976). For example, a child may have discovered a pattern or formula for expressing possession, 'possessor + thing possessed', but at first would use this only with a limited number of possessors (perhaps *mummy*, *daddy*) and a limited number of possessions (such as *shoe*, *coat*), as in *daddy shoe*, *mummy shoe*, *daddy coat*. These formulaic patterns seem to be based on meaning, and children possibly move over to an understanding of linguistic structure at a later stage, though the question of when true 'grammar' begins is a controversial issue. (See also **child language**.)

linguistic relativity see **Sapir–Whorf hypothesis**

linguistic representation vs access route see **access route vs linguistic representation**

lobes see **brain**

localisation (of language) The attempt to specify which areas of the brain handle language. The location of language within the brain is agreed on in outline, but is highly controversial in its details. In the majority of human beings, language is located in the left hemisphere (half) of the **brain**. Within this, speech production is controlled mainly by anterior (forward) portions of the brain, and is

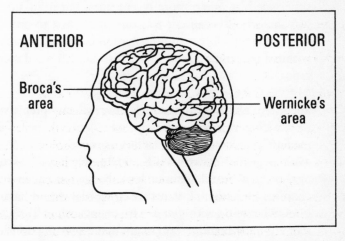

Fig. 3   Possible location of speech areas in the brain

traditionally associated with a location known as **Broca's area**. Speech comprehension is controlled mainly by posterior (back) regions, and is traditionally associated with **Wernicke's area**. However, there seems to be considerable individual variation, and some people argue that connections within the brain are more important than exact locations. Broca's area is linked to Wernicke's area by a bundle of nerve fibres known as the **arcuate fasciculus**. (See also **brain**.)

logogen model A model of word recognition which was influential in the 1970s, proposed by the British psychologist John Morton, The name comes from the Greek, meaning 'word birth'. Perceptual information is fed into the logogen system, which contains a logogen for each word. When the information reaches a certain critical level, the logogen 'fires', and the word is 'born'. A frequently used word would require less perceptual information, whereas a rare one would require rather more before it reached the critical level. This model has now been superseded by other, more recent ones, but in its time it was important because it was one of the first to propose how different sources of information could be combined within a recognition model. (See also **model; word recognition**.)

lookahead An ability within models of speech comprehension to examine words beyond the ones that are being immediately processed. This facility is required in order to avoid repeated backtracking (moving back and starting again). In a model without lookahead, the parser (mechanism for assigning structure to words) would have to guess what to do with *that* in a fragment such as *Tony saw that . . .*, for example, and might make a wrong decision, resulting in backtracking. But a parser with lookahead could distinguish in advance between *Tony saw that pig* and *Tony saw that the pig was angry*. A limited lookahead seems to be required in order to simulate the comprehension ability of humans, who probably backtrack only occasionally, mainly when they encounter **garden-path sentences**. (See also **parsing**; **speech comprehension**.)

lying The ability to talk convincingly about something entirely fictitious, with no back-up circumstantial evidence. This deliberate use of language as a tool requires an ability to deceive, a fairly advanced skill, by ape standards. Successful lying requires a person to have a **theory of mind**, the capacity to understand a situation from another person's point of view. Children suffering from the disorder of *autism* appear not to be able to do this.

M

malapropism A speech or writing error in which a word similar in sound to the intended one is uttered, as in *The cold is being exasperated* (exacerbated) *by the wind*. The name comes from Mrs. Malaprop, a character in Richard Sheridan's play *The Rivals* (1775), who kept muddling up words, as in *My affluence* (influence) *over my niece is very small*; *Few gentlemen nowadays know how to value the ineffectual* (intellectual) *qualities in a woman*. Mrs. Malaprop's mistakes were due to lack of knowledge, and errors caused by ignorance are sometimes known as 'classical malapropisms' in order to distinguish them from temporary **slips of the tongue** (speech errors), in which a person knows the correct form but has mistakenly uttered the wrong one. A malapropism is a common kind of **selection error** (selection of a wrong word) and provides some insight into how people find words. They show that speakers pay considerable attention to the beginnings and endings, and also to the word rhythm, suggesting that word finding might be a procedure in which word outlines are found first, then the details filled in later. (See also **word retrieval**.)

Marta A pseudonym for **Laura**, a severely retarded American female whose speech is fluent and richly structured. **Laura** is unable to carry out sorting tasks easily done by a two-year old, such as separating pictures of humans from objects; yet her speech contains numerous complex structures, as in *He was saying that I lost my battery-powered watch that I loved*, even though she quite often fails to make sense, as in *I was sixteen last year and now I'm nineteen this year*. Her speech suggests that an ability to use language structure is separate from general cognitive abilities, though these are needed in order to produce meaningful speech. (See also **chatterbox syndrome, cognitive abilities; innateness; modularity**.)

maturationally controlled behaviour Behaviour whose development is biologically regulated, such as sexual behaviour and walking, which emerge at roughly similar times in all humans in normal circumstances. Language is now thought to be an example of this type of behaviour, which has a number of distinct characteristics, according to Eric **Lenneberg** (1967): (1) regularity in the order of appearance of particular milestones (stages), which can normally be correlated with age and other aspects of development; (2) a relatively stable surrounding environment, which the child uses differently as he or she develops; (3) emergence of the behaviour before it is of any immediate use to the individual; (4) the beginnings of the behaviour are not just clumsy attempts to attain a particular goal. The important point is that in a normal environment something internal in the child causes the behaviour to unfold. It cannot therefore be radically speeded up, so intensive teaching is unlikely to help. It can, however, be temporarily slowed down, if the environment is unsatisfactory – if, for example, a child heard very little speech. Recently, the notion of **guided learning** has become important for understanding the development of genetically programmed behaviour. (See also **child language**.)

mean length of utterance (MLU) The average length of an utterance, normally calculated in morphemes (minimal grammatical units). *Cats drink milk* would count as four morphemes *Cat-s drink milk*. This provides a rough guide to the stage of linguistic development of a child, even though it is not an accurate measure of progress: a child who has learned long phrases by rote might score higher than another who was working from productive rules. (See also **child language; rule**.)

mental lexicon The word-store in the human mind. The human lexicon is fairly different in nature from printed dictionaries, though exactly how words are stored is still under discussion. There is a long-lasting controversy over whether words such as *faithful* and *goodness*, are listed as wholes, or broken down into morphemes (minimal grammatical units) *faith*, *-ful*, *good*, *-ness*, which are then assembled. Recent research suggests that words are mostly stored as wholes, but that word endings such as plural *-s* and past tense *-d* are added on in the course of speech. An additional word formation component possibly enables humans to break down words into morphemes in order to form new ones. (See also **word recognition; word retrieval**.)

mental model see **model**

mentalese The language of thought. The term is particularly associated with the work of the American psychologist Jerry Fodor, who argued in *The language of thought* (1975) that mentalese is very like human language, in that humans normally think in terms of their language, rather than in some deeply abstract or highly fragmented set of semantic features. (See also **semantic feature theory**.)

meronymy Also known as partonymy. The relationship between parts and wholes, as fingers are part of a hand, a hand is part of an arm, and so on, from the Greek word *meros* 'part'. Meronymy seems to be important for speakers of a language, in the way they relate words to one another, but it has not been studied systematically, and has been given a lower priority than logical relationships such as the link between subordinates and their *superordinates* (e.g. a *tulip* is a *flower*). Meronymy seems to be primarily a relationship between nouns, and is one factor that has led to the realisation that different parts of speech (word classes) are treated differently in the mental lexicon. A problem arises in that meronymy boundaries are not clearcut. Everyone agrees that a finger as part of a hand is a good example of meronymy, but researchers disagree over borderline cases. Is a punchline a part of a joke, for example?

metalinguistic ability The ability to think and reason about language, as opposed to using it. In general, metalinguistic ability lags behind correct usage. For example, a child might produce correct sentences such as *John ate the orange, and the dog ate the biscuit*, long before he or she was able to explain the linguistic 'rules' involved: 'Proper names in English do not normally occur with a determiner (a word such as *a*, *the*, *this*), but a determiner normally precedes common nouns such as *dog* in the singular.'

metaphor Metaphor is 'the application of one thing to a name belonging to another', according to the classical definition by the ancient Greek philosopher Aristotle, as in 'Henry's a dinosaur', presumably meaning that Henry is old-fashioned – though this 'classical' definition is now regarded as out-of-date. At one time, metaphor was regarded as a literary decoration which affected single words. In recent years the study of metaphor has become a major part of **cognitive linguistics**. Metaphors are pervasive in ordinary conversation, and it is impossible to talk about some topics, particularly those involving human senses and perception, without using metaphors, as in *bristle with rage, an elegant wine, glowing praise, soft music, warm words*. Dull topics also tend to be livened up with metaphor, so the financial pages of newspapers contain dozens, as in *economic meltdown, falling pound*. Some metaphors reflect **image schemata** which may be universal, as the notion that *up* is good and *down* is bad, e.g. *to go up in the world, to be down in the dumps*. The human body is perennially a major source of metaphor, and the origin of many everyday terms. Words are coined with reference to parts of the body, as in *the foot of the mountain, the heart of the matter*, and also with reference to actions, as in *to see the meaning, to grasp an argument*. Other metaphors may be long-term cultural ones, such as anger envisaged as heated fluid in a container, e.g. *he was brimming with rage, you make my blood boil*. The dominant technology of the day often forms short-lived metaphors, as in the widespread use of computer-related metaphors. The importance of metaphor is that it shows that humans build for themselves **idealised cognitive models (ICMs)** in the terminology of George Lakoff, one of the pioneers of metaphor studies. Such ICMs, which may or may not match external 'reality', provide the means by which humans make sense of the world they live in.

metathesis see **exchange error**

metonymy A figure of speech in which part of a person or object is used in place of a whole person or object, e.g.'We need some *fresh faces*' (new people); 'We want an *extra pair of hands*' (another helper). The metonym is usually adjacent to the person or object which it replaces. It therefore expresses a relationship of contiguity, as opposed to **metaphor** where the relationship is typically one of substitution.

metrical tree A diagram which shows the metrical pattern of a word. In English, 'strong' and 'weak' syllables typically alternate, e.g. *condescension*. Such a pattern appears to play a role in memory for words, especially in children. (See also **rhythm**.)

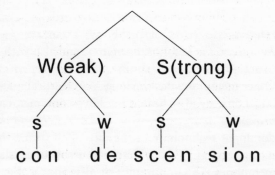

Fig. 4   A metrical tree

MID see **multi-infarct dementia**

milestones (in language acquisition) see **child language; order of acquisition**

mind, theory of The capacity to understand a situation from another person's point of view. Other primates, and children suffering from the disorder of *autism* appear not to be able to do this. Successful **lying** shows that someone has a theory of mind.

mindblindness The label given to someone who does not have a **theory of mind**. (See **mind, theory of.**)

minimal attachment (principle of) A proposed **speech comprehension** strategy: 'Link each new item to the preceding ones by means of the simplest structures possible.' For example, anyone hearing the words *The cow kicked . . .* would be likely to assume that the cow is kicking something, rather than the more complex but possible alternative, that the cow is being kicked, as in *The cow kicked by the donkey became uncontrollable.* This broad strategy is regarded by some researchers as one which includes and explains the **canonical sentoid strategy**, the imposition of the standard (canonical) form of a sentence. In general, the role of **perceptual strategies** (rule-of-thumb procedures) in **parsing** (assignment of structure to groups of words in comprehension) is still unclear, since they interact with lexical knowledge in ways not yet fully understood.

minimalist program Recent suggestions by **Chomsky** on the bare bones of language. These differ radically from his earlier proposals for a **transformational grammar**. He argues that the apparent diversity of languages is illusory, and that linguistic differences are the result of fixed principles under slightly varying conditions. The minimalist program retains his suggestions for **parameter setting**, in which a child learning language 'sets parameters' via switches, which can be set in one of two positions. It also contains outline proposals for some overall principles, which are mostly ones of 'economy' or simplicity. For example, if one of two chunks of structure needs to be moved, then the one which moves least far must be selected, in a principle labelled 'Shortest Move.'

MLU see **mean length of utterance**

model (of language) A representation of language which attempts to incorporate its essential features. Such models are guesses or hypotheses about the nature of language. Some models of language try to represent the internalised grammar of a person who knows the language, others try to specify the processes of speech production and speech comprehension. Models of **word recognition** and **parsing** (assignment of structure to groups of words) are perhaps the most common. Parsing models, such as **ATNs**, are particularly widespread, because they can be implemented on a computer. A model of language produced by a researcher is different from a *cognitive model* or *mental model* which refers to a representation which exists in someone's mind. Such mental models might not have any 'real' existence. For example, many English people have a mental model of a *week*, consisting of seven days, composed of five working days followed by two free days. This is a purely conventional notion, but the model influences their behaviour, so can be regarded as having **psychological reality**.

modularity (of language) The property of being composed of separate 'modules' or components. Some linguists believe language is 'modular' in the sense that it is a self-contained system within the mind, which is largely independent of general intelligence. They also believe that there are semi-independent modules within the language system. The metaphor is inspired by computer programs, which are often composed of fairly simple separate subsystems which interact to produce a complex output. Within language, the question of modules is controversial, and so is the question of whether (if they exist) they are genetically inbuilt, or developed over time. But the notion of a language module which is distinct from general cognitive abilities is supported by the discovery of severely mentally subnormal children such as **Marta,** who speak fluently, though without making much sense: *It was no ordinary school, it was just good old no buses.* (See also **innateness.**)

monitoring device A checking mechanism, which examines whether speech output is correct. Humans are presumed to use such a device when they produce speech, partly because they are often able to correct mistakes they have made: *Par cark, sorry, I meant car park.* But there is also evidence for a subconscious monitoring device working in the case of **slips of the tongue** (unintended speech errors), since these form real words more often than would be expected by chance, as in *lowing the morn* (mowing the lawn), *peach seduction* (speech production). This suggests that the human mind might be checking that the output contains real words, even though speakers are not normally aware of this process. (See also **speech production.**)

motor theory (of speech perception) A hypothesis that, in order to perceive sounds, humans have subconsciously to produce them. The term 'motor', here, is used in the sense of 'producing'. For example, in order to perceive a sound [p], a hearer would have to mentally form [p], then match the subconsciously produced sound against what was heard. This theory is also called *analysis-by-synthesis*, because hearers analyze the sounds heard by subconsciously assembling (synthesising) them. At one time, this viewpoint was highly influential, but is now thought by many researchers to be unlikely. (See also **speech perception**.)

motor vs sensory Connected with outgoing movement versus incoming sensation. The 'motor cortex' is the area in the brain which controls voluntary movement, whereas the 'sensory cortex' is that part of the brain which handles incoming sensations. 'Motor' **aphasia** describes a serious disorder relating to speech production, and 'sensory' **aphasia** describes a serious problem relating to speech comprehension, though these terms are now considered somewhat old-fashioned, and the terms **expressive aphasia** and **receptive aphasia** are more usual. (See also **brain**.)

movement error A slip of the tongue (speech error) in which a sound, syllable or word is moved out of its expected place. Also known as an **assemblage error**, since the speech has been correctly selected, but wrongly assembled.

multi-infarct dementia A condition in which a person's memory is destroyed by multiple mini-strokes, sometimes confused with **Alzheimer's disease** (DAT).

multilingual see **bilingualism**

multiple activation The view that humans activate a range of words, both in **word recognition** and **word retrieval**, before selecting the one they want. The **cohort model**

was one of the first to build this into a psycholinguistic theory.

[N]

naming insight The realisation by children that words are 'names' for things. According to some researchers, this realisation does not necessarily develop until around the age of fifteen months, although a few children appear to acquire it at a younger age. Those who do not possess the 'naming insight' are still able to name things apparently satisfactorily, but to them it is merely a kind of game, in which an object such as a car is responded to with a given sound [ka:], when an adult points to it. (See also **child language**.)

nature vs nurture controversy A long-standing argument as to whether language is innately pre-programmed in the same way as walking, or whether it is learned in the same way as typewriting or sewing. It is also known as a distinction between 'hard-wired' and 'soft-wired' behaviour. At one time, it was thought that human and animal behaviour could be neatly divided into these two types. Recently, it has become clear that the divide is an oversimplification, and that natural behaviour requires a considerable amount of careful nurture, and that nurtured behaviour is impossible without an innate predisposition. Nowadays this controversy has to a large extent been replaced by the notion of **guided learning**, the idea that innate guidelines allow some types of behaviour to be learned relatively easily. Such behaviour is likely to be **maturationally controlled** (biologically programmed).

negative evidence Information presented to a child that his or her linguistic form is wrong. The term became particularly common in the phrase 'no negative evidence', which summarises the claim that children receive relatively little negative evidence, and may not pay much attention to that which they do receive. Parents tend to correct children's statements for truthfulness and politeness, more than they correct grammar (*No, Uncle came this afternoon, not this morning*; *say thank you*), and children often ignore instructions such as: *Say took, not taked*. This raises the problem of **learnability**, how children manage to learn language, and in particular how they are able to correct their mistakes. Various proposals have been made as to how children handle this, such as appeals to innate principles: for example, the so-called **uniqueness principle** suggests that children follow a principle of 'one form, one meaning', and drop their own wrong form when they realise another one is used by everyone else with the same meaning as their own. Some recent work suggests that children do, after all, pay careful attention to what is said to them, including negative evidence, but only in certain circumstances. Mostly, they attend to aspects of speech which they are currently monitoring and working on – though there seems to be considerable differences between children as to how much they listen carefully to those who are talking to them.

neologism A newly coined word. The term is applied to new words which enter language by normal routes, and also to meaningless words, such as *landocks*, *bandicks*, typically coined by patients suffering from **fluent aphasia**.

neoteny The extended childhood enjoyed by humans, from the Greek words for 'young-stretch'. Compared with most animals, human youngsters spend a long time being looked after by adults. During this lengthy learning period, they receive protracted stimulation from the adults around, and their brains retain their youthful flexibility.

network An interconnected system. The word 'network' is most often combined with another word specifying the particular kind of network involved, as in 'semantic network'. (See also **semantic network theory**.)

network models see **connectionism**

neurolinguistics A branch of linguistics concerned with the relationship between the brain and linguistic processing. Neurolinguistics attempts to locate areas within the brain which are closely related to speech, and to map blood-flow patterns in the brain as speech is spoken or heard. It overlaps with clinical linguistics, which deals with patients suffering from **aphasia** and other speech disorders. (See also **brain; brain scans; localisation.**)

neurons see **brain**

neuropsychology see **brain vs mind**

Nicaraguan signing community A deaf community which has developed a full signed language with remarkable rapidity. A partial signed language was in use around twenty years ago, and this was picked up and elaborated on by a younger generation. Talented individuals have played a major role: for example, a young deaf boy called Santos learned rudimentary signing from his deaf aunt and uncle, but soon progressed beyond them. This community shows how efficiently language can be transferred to another medium, if the normal spoken route is unavailable, and how fast a novel language system can be developed, if a group of interacting individuals exist to reinforce and extend it.

Nim Chimpsky An ape taught sign language by Herbert Terrace at Columbia University, New York, in the 1970s. Nim's achievements were fairly similar to those of better known apes, such as **Washoe**. (See also **ape signing**.)

O

one-word utterances see **holophrase**

ontogeny vs philogeny The course of the development of an individual as opposed to the course of development of the species. In the mid-nineteenth century, Ernst Heinrich Haeckel, a German sociologist, proposed that 'ontogeny recapitulates philogeny', the notion that a maturing individual rapidly repeats the changes found slowly over the millenia in the species. This idea was immensely popular, and is still occasionally repeated today. But it is false. Ontogeny occasionally recapitulates philogeny, but does not necessarily do so.

open-endedness see **creativity**

operant conditioning Training by means of voluntary responses, since an 'operant' is a voluntary response, rather than an automatic one. This is essentially 'trial by error' learning, a type of training which is highly successful with rats and pigeons. A rat learns by experimenting that, if it presses a bar, it gets some food. Then, the task is made more difficult: it only gets food if it presses the bar while a light is flashing. The psychologist B. F. Skinner, a strong advocate of this approach, known generally as **behaviourism**, claimed in his book *Verbal Behavior* (1957) that this type of procedure could be extended to human language. Noam **Chomsky** first became widely known when he wrote a damning review of this book (1959), showing that language acquisition could not be explained in this way, and that the supposed parallels between rats and humans were an illusion.

operating principles A number of self-instructions which children follow in order to work out the structure of language, such as 'Pay attention to the ends of words', 'Pay attention to the order of words', according to the American psychologist Dan Slobin. Slobin's proposals were first made in the early 1970s, when he suggested relatively few operating principles. Since then, he has progressively added to them, which presents a problem: there are now so many that some of them clash. Therefore, unless some guiding overall principles become clear, the whole theory is in danger of becoming meaningless. (See also **order of acquisition**.)

optimality theory A theory of grammar which is gaining an increasing number of supporters. Unlike **Chomsky**, whose theories propose fixed **constraints** on human language, proponents of optimality theory argue that all constraints are potentially violable. Languages differ, partly because they rank these constraints in different ways. Optimality theory has been shown to be of great interest for phonology (sound structure), though researchers are still arguing about its relevance to syntax.

order of acquisition The order in which children acquire sounds and constructions. This is similar among widely separated children, though not identical. Most children **coo** (utter *goo-goo* sounds) at around six weeks, then **babble** (utter repeated syllables such as *ma-ma-ma, ba-ba-ba*) at around six months. There is no universal order of acquisition of sounds, as was once thought, but it is usual for sounds which require relatively little muscular control (such as [b]) to be produced early, so there are similarities across children. Children begin uttering single words at around a year, and start putting two words together at around eighteen months, though there is considerable individual variation. They begin to acquire morphological structures (word endings and 'little words' such as *is*) at around the age of two years. The order in which word endings are acquired tends to be similar among those who speak the same language. Some linguistic structures seem to be easier for children to grasp than others. For example, those in two parts as in *Polly is playing* (where *is* and *-ing* are separated by the verb) are acquired relatively late. Various proposals have been made to explain the reasons underlying the order of development of morphology. Among the best known are the **operating principles** proposed by the American psychologist Dan Slobin, and the **competition model** put forward by the American Brian MacWhinney. Various other factors need to be taken into consideration, such as the speech addressed to children (**caregiver language**), and possible innate programming. (See also **acquisition; child language; innateness; two-word stage.**)

origin of language The beginning stages of language have finally become an acceptable linguistic area of study, after centuries of neglect and disapproval. All human languages are now thought to have come from a single source, possibly located in East Africa. The date is less certain, though must have been before 50,000 BP in order to account for the spread of language round the world.

overactivation The notion, now widely accepted, that humans mentally consider numerous words for recognition or production, then narrow them down to the one required. The **cohort model** is one such theory.

overextension see **overgeneralisation**

overgeneralisation The extension of a word or rule beyond its normal limit. It occurs in child language, when children might use *duck* for any bird which swims, including ducks, seagulls and swans. They also extend word endings, saying such things as *breaked* for 'broke', and *taked* for 'took'. Overgeneralisations show that children are not just imitating adults, but are devising their own rules to handle language. In practice, overgeneralisations are not as common as *undergeneralisations*, when children underextend a word or ending, though these are not usually detected, because they tend to be used in the correct circumstances. For example, a child who pointed to a robin and said 'look at that bird' might think that 'bird' was the name for 'robin'. The relatively small number of overgeneralisations has led some researchers to doubt their existence, and to propose a **subset principle**, which suggests that children always select the smallest possible rule, which they then expand; however, this cannot be completely right, because overgeneralisations do in fact occur. A major difficulty raised by overgeneralisation is the **retreat problem** – how children move back from overly general rules.

P

P and P see **principles and parameters**

paragrammatism see **fluent aphasia**

parallel distributed processing (PDP) see **connectionism**

parallel function strategy A possible **speech comprehension** strategy: 'Assume that the subject of the main clause is also the subject of any subordinate clause'. In a sentence such as: *Peter phoned Paul when he got back from holiday*, the assumption is that it was Peter, rather than Paul, who had returned from holiday. This strategy is thought to be a fairly weak one, since it can easily be overridden by other factors, as in: *Peter phoned Paul because he was ill*, where many people assume that Paul is the person who is ill, on the assumption that sick people receive more phone calls than they initiate. The whole role of **perceptual strategies** (rule-of-thumb procedures) within **parsing** (the assignment of structure to groups of words in comprehension) is a controversial one, since they interact with numerous other factors.

parallel vs serial processing A question concerning the simultaneous (parallel) versus the sequential (serial) processing of language. When recognising a word, do hearers check out several possibilities simultaneously (a parallel process)? Or do they match what they hear against words one after the other, perhaps starting with the most frequently used ones (a serial process)? In recent years, it has become clear that the human mind is capable of multiple parallel processing, which accounts to some extent for the speed with which humans can handle language. There have been recent attempts to simulate parallel processing on computers, under the general heading **connectionism**.

parameter setting A theory of child language acquisition which claims that children have a prior knowledge of some crucial options available to languages. They then select those which fit in with the language to which they are exposed. A 'parameter' can be defined as an essential property which can be set at various values: for example, temperature is a parameter of the atmosphere. Parameter setting in language was first proposed by the American linguist Noam **Chomsky**. He suggested that it might work by 'switches' which can be set in one of two positions. For example, children might expect languages to require pronouns in front of verbs as in English *I am cold*, or not, as in Italian *Sono freddo* 'am cold', an option known as the *pro-drop parameter* (pronoun-dropping parameter). Choice of one of these options has repercussions throughout the language, and children might automatically know these. In practice, parameter setting as it was first proposed is unlikely to work. But it is an interesting (though incomplete) attempt to specify how the notion of **guided learning** might work in humans, and also how they achieve consistency within a language.

parole see **competence vs performance**

parrot see **Alex**

parsing The assignment of structure to word sequences in the process of **speech comprehension**. Many researchers agree in outline on the processes involved, but argue strongly about their relative importance. Some researchers argue that hearers listen for outline clues, and then jump to conclusions (a **perceptual strategy** approach). Others claim that hearers mostly work through a sentence in a systematic way, assigning structure to each word as they come to it, holding any unassigned word in memory until a place is found for it (sometimes called a **left-to-right** approach, found for example in **ATNs**). The relationship between syntax (rules of structure), the lexicon (vocabulary) and world knowledge is also disputed. Some researchers argue that syntax initially has priority. Others claim that all types of processing are interwoven right from the start, a view that appears to be winning out.

partonymy see **meronymy**

pause A temporary stop in speech. Pauses may be *silent* or *filled*, as in *er-er*, *um-um*. They occur for various reasons, such as breathing, speech planning and word searching. There is controversy over the exact interpretation of pausing phenomena, though researchers generally agree that pauses occur within clauses, rather than between them. This suggests that speakers begin planning the next clause while still uttering the current one. (See also **speech production**.)

PDP see **connectionism**

perception see **speech perception**

perceptual strategies Informed guesses which hearers may use as they comprehend sentences. According to this viewpoint, hearers listen for outline clues, and then jump to conclusions about what they are hearing. For example, anyone hearing the words *The cow pushed . . .* might immediately jump to the conclusion that the cow is doing the pushing, even though this might be wrong, if the sentence turns out to be *The cow pushed through the hedge put up quite a fight*. This particular strategy is known as the **canonical sentoid strategy** (the assumption that a sentence follows the 'normal' or canonical form of most English sentences). Some other proposed strategies are the **parallel function strategy**, the **principle of late closure**, and the **principle of minimal attachment**. The strategy approach to **parsing** (the assignment of structure to groups of words during speech comprehension) was particularly widespread in the 1970s, when attempts were made to propose strategies which might be valid across different language types. More recently, it has been supplemented by other approaches. (See also **speech comprehension**.)

perseveration An error in which a sound, syllable or word is mistakenly repeated in speaking, writing or signing. For example: *chew chew* (two) *tablets, a thin chin . . . er cheese pizza*. Among normal speakers, there are relatively few errors of this type, but they are common in certain types of **aphasia**. This suggests that speakers normally 'wipe off' items they have prepared for utterance as soon as they have used them. Perseverations, also known as *repetitions*, are a type of **assemblage error**, in that items selected for production have been wrongly ordered. Such **slips of the tongue** (speech errors) are a major source of evidence for understanding speech production mechanisms. Similarly, **slips of the pen** and **slips of the hand** provide information about the processes underlying writing and signing. (See also **speech production**.)

PET scan see **positron emission tomography**

philogeny vs ontogeny see **ontogeny vs philogeny**

phoneme monitoring An experimental technique in which someone is asked to listen for a particular sound, as in: 'Press this button when you hear the sound [b]'. The assumption is that this task is likely to be easier if the words directly preceding the 'target' sound are easy to comprehend. In this way, researchers can measure complexity of processing. For example, it has been shown that an ambiguous word such as *port* (drink or harbour?) causes a delay in detecting the required phoneme, suggesting that hearers may subconsciously have noted the ambiguity, even when they are not consciously aware of doing so. (See also **ambiguity; experimental psycholinguistics.**)

phonological recoding hypothesis The proposal that reading involves 'translating' the written words into sounds, either silently or aloud. This is assumed to be done by **grapheme–phoneme correspondence rules.** The extent to which this is done is a source of controversy among those who study reading. In general, the faster and more skilled the reader, the less likely they are to phonologically recode what they are reading.

phonology see **grammar**

Pinker, Steven An American psychologist, Professor in the Department of Brain and Cognitive Sciences at the Massachusetts Insititute of Technology. He has written extensively on language, and his best known book *The language instinct* (1994) has done much to spread knowledge of language to a wider audience, especially an understanding that an ability to handle language is part of the biological make-up of the human brain.

pivot grammar A simple grammatical system in which an utterance 'pivots' around a small set of recurring words. In the early 1960s, this type of grammar was claimed to be universal for children at the **two-word stage.** For example, a child might have the pivot words *want, allgone, see,* and *bye-bye,* and be able to attach these to a large number of different nouns, so producing utterances such as: *allgone shoe, want mummy, see doggie.* However, only a few children have a genuine pivot grammar. Most others have some utterances with a 'pivot look', such as *hi mommy,* but have in addition a large number of other combinations which cannot be accounted for by a pivot construction.

planning see **speech planning**

polysemy Multiple meanings. Most words have more than one meaning. *Hand*, for example, can mean not only 'the extremity of the arm', but also 'applause', as in *Give her a good hand*; 'aid' as in *Lend me a hand*; 'skill requiring practice' as in *I must keep my hand in*; 'a set of cards' as in *He was dealt a good hand*. At one time, changed meanings were thought of as 'weakening'. But this is unrealistic, because the original meaning usually remains, alongside the extra meanings. Work on polysemy has led to a greater understanding of the mechanisms underlying semantic change.

positron emission tomography (PET scanning) A type of **brain scan**, which uses radioactive isotopes to measure changes in the brain's activity as it performs tests of various kinds. It is useful for identifying which portions of the brain are active during various linguistic tasks.

pragmatics The study of 'speaker meaning', the interpretations given to utterances by speakers, which are not necessarily the same as the literal linguistic meanings. The linguistic meaning of *empty cup*, for example, is 'a drinking container which does not contain anything'. But someone who said, 'My cup's empty', would probably 'mean' *Please will you pour me another cup of coffee*. Pragmatics is therefore important for **interpretation**, one of the processes involved in **speech comprehension**. The **co-operative principle**, and **speech act theory** are two viewpoints which have been influential in pragmatics in recent years.

prefix stripping A claim that people remove prefixes from the beginning of complex words when they comprehend them. For example, on coming across a word such as *include*, hearers might mentally remove *in-*, and 'look up' the sequence *-clude* in their mental lexicon. It now seems unlikely that this happens, since recent research suggests that people mostly store words as wholes. (See also **mental lexicon**.)

priming A technique used in experimental studies, in which a person is prepared for a subsequent word or utterance. The word *winter* might 'prime' the word *snow*, for example, in that after hearing *winter* a person would be likely to recognise *snow* more quickly in a **lexical decision task** (deciding whether a sequence of sounds or letters is a word or not). If a word is found to prime another, then the words could be closely connected in the mind. This technique is therefore used to find out about such links. (See also **experimental psycholinguistics**.)

principle of contrast see **uniqueness principle**

principle of late closure see **late closure**

principle of minimal attachment see **minimal attachment**

principles and parameters (also known as **P and P**) An approach to language proposed by the linguist Noam **Chomsky**. He suggests that children are innately endowed with an understanding of some basic linguistic principles, and also a knowledge of some crucial options available to languages. They then select those which fit in with the language to which they are exposed. This process is known as **parameter setting**.

principles vs rules see **rule**

pro-drop see **parameter setting**

production see **speech production**

productive processes see **productivity**

productivity The ability of language speakers to produce an indefinite number of new utterances, also known as **creativity** or **open-endedness**. The term is often used more narrowly, in relation to word formation. A word-formation process is productive if it is used as a pattern for coining new words, as with the suffix -*ness*, which can nowadays be attached not only to new words, as *upfrontness*, but also to phrases as in *up-to-dateness*.

prototype theory A hypothesis that people understand the meaning of words by reference to a highly typical example. A robin is regarded as a prototypical bird by many, for example, so the word *bird* would be thought of as involving a creature with many robin-like characteristics, such as feathers, ability to fly, nest-building habit, and so on, rather than a penguin, which although still a bird, is not a prototypical one. Humans are fairly reliable in their ability to rank items according to how typical they are, in that there is widespread agreement between speakers within the same culture. But there is still considerable controversy as to what mental prototypes truly represent, as they seem to involve a mixture of characteristics used for identification, and traits involving knowledge not predictable from appearance only. In some cases, the notion of prototype involves the setting up of a complete mental model, an **ICM** or **frame**, as in the case of the word *week*, which to many people involves the cultural notion of five working days followed by two days rest.

psycholinguistics The study of language and the mind, primarily how humans understand, produce, store, and acquire language. It is sometimes distinguished from the *psychology of language*, a wider field which involves somewhat broader questions, such as the extent to which language influences thought. A broader field still is the *psychology of communication*, which includes all human communication, including facial expressions and gestures. Psycholinguistics can be studied from a number of different viewpoints, using a variety of methods. **Experimental psycholinguistics** finds out about language by means of carefully controlled experiments. **Cognitive psycholinguistics** tends to reach conclusions about language mechanisms by means of reasoning. **Developmental psycholinguistics** refers to the study of the development of language in children, and uses both observations and experiments. Psycholinguistics overlaps with **neurolinguistics**, the study of language and the brain. (See also **child language**.)

psychological reality problem The task of assessing to what extent academic theories present a true account of the situation in the human mind or brain. The problem was much discussed when **Chomsky** first proposed the notion of a **transformational grammar**, which at one time was presumed by some people to be a possible model of speech comprehension and speech production. The **correspondence hypothesis** and the **derivational theory of complexity** were hypotheses which attempted to test this, though the result was negative. Chomsky himself never claimed that his grammar was a model of speech processes, merely that it 'captured' relationships between various linguistic constructions.

psychology of communication see **psycholinguistics**

psychology of language see **psycholinguistics**

Pustejovsky, James An American linguist who in his book *The generative lexicon* (1995) drew attention to the complexity of the mental lexicon, and the extensiveness of **polysemy**. He argues that the lexicon is an active and central component of human linguistic ability.

Q

qualia structure The subjective feelings associated with consciousness, such as the experience of the blueness of blue, the itchiness of an itch, the painfulness of pain. **Pustejovksy** proposes that such feelings should be brought into a model of the **mental lexicon**.

R

reading see **grapheme–phoneme correspondence rules; phonological recoding hypothesis**.

recasts Reformulation of speech, usually a child's utterance rephrased by an adult. A child might say: *doggie dinner*, for example, to which an adult might respond: *Yes, it's time to give the dog something to eat*. Recasts are sometimes contrasted with **expansions**, which simply enlarge on the child's utterance, as in *doggie dinner* expanded to 'Yes, the doggie wants his dinner'. Recasts by **caregivers** (those looking after children) are sometimes claimed to be particularly helpful for language acquisition. (See also **caregiver speech**.)

receptive aphasia see **aphasia; expressive vs receptive aphasia; motor vs sensory**

recognition see **word recognition**

recursiveness (also **recursion**) The property of language which enables it to repeatedly re-run the same construction, by re-applying the same rules, as in *This is the cat, that killed the rat, that ate the malt . . .* and so on. Its importance lies in the fact that it is impossible ever to specify all sentences of a language, because the possibility of recursion means that the list would be endless.

regression hypothesis A suggestion that people with speech disorders 'unlearn' language in the reverse order to that in which children acquire it. The theory first appeared in 1883 as 'Ribot's Law' after the Frenchmen who proposed it. In the early 1940s, it was put forward by the linguist Roman **Jakobson**, in relation to speech sounds. The hypothesis turned out to be false, even though there are some superficial similarities between child language and disordered speech. For example, some sounds, such as [m], require less muscular control than others: these occur early in child language, and are often retained in speech disorders. But the dissimilarities are greater than the similarities. (See also **aphasia**.)

repair The 'mending' of an utterance which was felt to be unsatisfactory. The repair can be carried out either by the person who produced the unsatisfactory utterance ('self-repair') as in *Peter cooked dinner, I mean breakfast*, or by someone else ('other repair'), as in *You said Peter, don't you mean David?'* Children's self-repairs provide useful information about their developing **metalinguistic ability** (conscious awareness of the linguistic system), as in *The boy met the girl, I mean, the boy met a girl*.

repetition see **perseveration**

replacement error A slip of the tongue (speech error) in which one word or sound is mistakenly used in place of another. Also known as a **selection error**, since a wrong item has been chosen.

retreat problem The question of how children learn to correct their overgeneralised forms, such as *taked* for 'took'. This is considered puzzling, because they do not necessarily pay attention to **negative evidence** (correction) by their parents. Some child language researchers have therefore proposed various internal mechanisms which might be at work in order to explain how language is learnable. (See also **caregiver language; learnability; overgeneralisation.**)

retrieval see **word retrieval**

retrieval vs storage Procedures used in word-finding, as opposed to the internal representation of a word. (See also **word recognition; word retrieval.**)

rhythm (of speech) A fixed 'biological beat' may underlie the ability of humans to sequence their utterances, though this might be set at various speeds, depending on the language and the individual. Some neurological disorders may lead to a disturbance of the underlying rhythmic beat. For example, Parkinson's disease sometimes leads to uncontrollable speech acceleration. A **metrical tree** is a diagram which can show the rhythm and stress patterns of a language.

Rosch, Eleanor The psychologist who initiated the study of **prototype theory.**

rule An observed regularity in linguistic behaviour, of which the speaker is usually unaware. For example, a child who is shown a picture of a made-up animal, and told it is a *wug*, might be able to identify two of them as *two wugs*. This shows that the child has a 'rule' for forming plurals in English, even though he or she is unlikely to have any conscious knowledge of it. Such behaviour indicates that children cannot be acquiring language just by imitating adults; they must be working out rules of their own. This is also shown by wrongly applied 'rules' (by adult standards), as when children say *taked* instead of 'took', or *buyed* instead of 'bought'. The American linguist Noam **Chomsky** has suggested that *principles* might replace large numbers of individual rules. For example, a rule that English verbs are followed by objects (*break a bottle*) and another rule that prepositions are followed by their objects (*in a bottle*) might be replaced by a single principle specifying that the most important word in a phrase (its *head*) precedes the other components. However, this proposal is controversial, as are many of Chomsky's ideas. (See also **parameter setting**.)

S

SAAD A simple active affirmative declarative sentence, as *The man caught a fish*; *The girl picked a flower*.

Sapir–Whorf hypothesis A claim that human thought is affected by the particular language spoken, put forward by the American linguist Edward Sapir (1881–1939) and later taken up by his student Benjamin Lee Whorf (1897–1941). According to Sapir, the 'real world' is to a large extent built up out of language habits. In his view, no two languages are sufficiently similar to build up the 'same' world, consequently 'The worlds in which different societies live are distinct worlds, not merely the same world with different labels attached'. This view is also known as *linguistic relativity*. Whorf claimed that the

American-Indian language Hopi represented time in a way quite different from European languages, consequently the Hopi must envisage time quite differently. This viewpoint has been shown to be unlikely. Nowadays, most people assume that language influences thought to some extent, but does not necessarily force it into certain grooves. Experimental evidence shows that colour terminology can affect people's judgments about colour: speakers of the Uto-Aztecan language Tarahumara, which has a single word covering both blue and green, performed differently from English speakers on some tasks when asked to group colour chips within this range. In addition, the use of supposedly generic *he* to refer to either a male or a female as in *When a doctor is in a hospital, he is usually working* has been shown to add to the invisibility of working women: students tested on such sentences assumed that the doctor was male.

scan-copier A possible mechanism used in speech production, which looks over words partially pre-prepared for utterance, and then 'copies' them into the correct slot in the final output. A slip of the tongue (speech error) such as *leak wink* (weak link), for example, suggests that the correct sounds had already been selected, but were then mistakenly copied from a mental 'slate' into the wrong place in the utterance. It is difficult to explain assemblage errors (misorderings) unless a mechanism such as a scan-copier exists. One reason for the mistakes may be that an auditory (sound) image in a person's mind has to be converted into a spoken form.

scans see brain scans

schizophrenic language The language of patients suffering from the mental disorder labelled *schizophrenia*. Some of them produce jumbled language sometimes called **word salads**.

scribble talk Indistinct talk produced by young children, which often preserves good intonation patterns, but is otherwise fairly meaningless babble, with only the occasional identifiable word slotted in. It is parallel to the kind of scribble children sometimes produce when they pretend they are writing. Children vary in the amount of scribble talk they produce, some of them have a lot, others much less.

script A stored memory of a typical sequence of events, such as having a bath, or visiting a restaurant. This notion overlaps with the idea of remembered frameworks (stored scenes). Scripts and **frames** appear to be needed by humans in order to interpret speech. (See also **internalised cognitive models; interpretation.**)

selection error A mistake in which a wrong item, usually a wrong word, has been selected, in speech, writing or signing. Also known as a **replacement error**. Selection errors can be divided into 'similar meaning errors', as in *We don't lie in bed all night* (day), 'similar sound errors' (**malapropisms**), as in *He has a fine autonomy* (anatomy), and errors which combine these, as in *They learnt a simplified jargon on trading vehicles* (vessels). A further category is **blends**, in which two words have been combined into one, as in *He was wearing gymsolls, ah, plimshoes* (gymshoes, plimsolls). Such **slips of the tongue** (speech errors) can provide important information about speech production. Selection errors are particularly useful for the light they shed on **word retrieval** (word finding). Similarly, selection errors found in **slips of the pen** and **slips of the hand** provide information about writing and signing.

semantic feature theory A theory that the meaning of words is split into semantic components. For example, *puppy* might have the components of CANINE, NON-ADULT. At one time, children's overgeneralisations of meaning, such as *dog* for all four-legged animals, were assumed to be because children had not yet learned sufficient semantic features to make all the necessary distinctions in their language. However, this theory cannot account for all meaning errors made by children, and recent theories of meaning suggest that semantic feature theory is unlikely to be correct. A form of **prototype theory** might be a better explanation of children's mistakes.

semantic network theory A theory that words are organised in an interconnected system linked by logical relationships. For example, a sparrow is a kind of bird, and a bird is a kind of animal. Both of these statements are examples of the relationship of inclusion. The original theory of this type suggested that it might be possible to measure the distance between words in the network, but more recent studies suggest that the network is far less fixed than was once assumed.

semantic roles see **thematic roles**

semantics see **grammar**

sensitive period A period in life when children seem particularly 'tuned in' to acquiring language. This may begin before birth, since a **high amplitude sucking** procedure shows that infants as young as four days old reportedly react to hearing their own language, but not other languages. Youngsters are particularly sensitive to language in the early years of their life, then this sensitivity gradually tails away, though never entirely. It is now thought that children pay attention to particular aspects of language, at particular ages, though these different periods of interest overlap. Children listen particularly to the sounds of language when they are very young. From around the age of two they begin to concentrate on the syntax (grammar), and after that on the vocabulary – an ability to learn new words lasts throughout life. This notion of an altering sensitive period has replaced an earlier proposal of a **critical period**, a rigid time within which language must be acquired.

serial processing see **parallel vs serial processing**

shadowing A psycholinguistic technique in which hearers speak aloud language which is being played into their ears through earphones. This enables psycholinguists to measure how fast humans recognise words. When shadowing, hearers normally correct minor mistakes in the original, such as changing *tomorrance* to 'tomorrow'. This demonstrates that speech comprehension is an active, rather than a passive process. (See also **speech comprehension**.)

shift error see **assemblage error**

short-term memory see **working memory**

sign language Language expressed via hand gestures. Sign language is a complete language system, though it is different from spoken speech or written language, because signing occurs in three-dimensional space, which affects its form. Signs stand for whole concepts, such as 'sad', 'intend', 'approximately', 'roller-skating', which can be linked together to express anything required by the signer. The two best known varieties are *American Sign Lan-*

guage (ASL) and *British Sign Language* (BSL). Signs are made by altering three main variables: hand shape, hand movement, and *signing space* (area in relation to the body). For example, the ASL signs for 'summer', 'ugly' and 'dry' are the same hand shape (closed hand with raised and hooked forefinger), but made in different signing spaces: 'summer' on the forehead, 'ugly' at the nose, and 'dry' on the chin. In South America, a **Nicaraguan signing community** of deaf individuals has developed a full signed language with remarkable speed in the last twenty or so years. **Slips of the hand** (signing errors) can provide useful information about the way signers plan and produce their signs. A highly simplified version of ASL has been taught to some animals, the most famous being the chimp **Washoe**. Genuine sign language is not the same as *finger spelling*, a somewhat slow system in which each letter of the alphabet has a different hand shape and movement.

signing space see **sign language**

silent pause see **pause**

SLI see **specific language impairment**

slip of the ear A mishearing, as in *get some ceiling paint* heard instead of 'sealing tape', *urban spice* heard instead of 'herb and spice'. Such errors have two possible sources: in some cases, they result from genuine misperceptions, as in *fan* heard instead of 'van'. In other cases, the hearer may have correctly heard part of the word, and then made wrong assumptions about the rest. This jumping to conclusions on the basis of outline clues is a normal process in **word recognition**, since speech is too fast for the human ear to grasp each sound. (See also **speech perception**.)

slip of the eye An error made in reading. Such errors often involve the intrusion of letters from other words around, particularly words ahead of those being read, as in *more chilly people* (more people to camps or chilly . . .). This suggests that people do not read word by word, but try to scan whole chunks. It also indicates that readers often leap to conclusions on the basis of outline clues, as also happens in the **perceptual strategies** used in listening to spoken speech.

slip of the hand An error in signing, when someone using sign language makes a sign other than that which he or she intended. For example, a man signed that he would like *cream and butter* in his coffee. When this was queried, he corrected this to 'cream and sugar'. The American Sign Language signs for *butter* and *sugar* are similar in hand shape and hand movement, but are made in different *signing spaces* (regions in relation to the body). Such slips provide important clues to the way in which signers plan and produce signs, in much the same way that **slips of the tongue** provide information about speech, and **slips of the pen** about written language. (See also **sign language.**)

slip of the pen A written error, in which someone writes a word, syllable or sound other than that intended. These errors fall into the same general categories as **slips of the tongue** (speech errors), but they have different frequencies of occurrence, possibly due to the slower speed of writing. For example, in writing, there are many more omissions, as in *shrig* (shrimp and egg), leading to a large number of *blends*, suggesting that the mind is often ahead of the pen. Additional errors are caused by visual similarity between letters, as in *make the babby* (baby) *happy*, with an anticipation of the double letter in *happy*, which was probably partly due to the similarity between written *b* and *p*. Slips of the pen provide evidence about the planning and production of written language, in much the same way that slips of the tongue furnish clues to speech, and **slips of the hand** give pointers to sign language.

slip of the tongue A speech error, in which a speaker utters a word, syllable or sound in a way other than he or she intended. Such errors can be divided into **selection** (or **replacement**) errors in which a wrong item, usually a word, has been selected, as in *The question he intended to answer* (ask) . . ., and **assemblage** (or **movement**) errors in which correctly selected items have been wrongly assembled, as in *Have you turned on the washdisher?* (dishwasher). Such errors slip into recurring patterns, and so provide important information about speech production. Slips of the tongue are errors in spoken speech, but **slips of the pen** (written errors) and **slips of the hand** (sign language errors) are also found. (See also **speech production; tongue-slip laws**.)

soft-wired vs hard-wired see **hard-wired vs soft-wired**

sound symbolism An association between the sound of a word and its meaning. Onomatopoeia (imitation of the sound associated with a word) is widespread in the languages of the world in particular semantic areas. Bird-names sometimes attempt to echo the bird's call, for example *cuckoo*, *whippoorwil*. Human bodily noises may represent the sound emitted, for example *burp*, *hiccup*, and so may inanimate sounds, for example *bang*, *plop*, *splash*. Words involving sucking often include the sequence *s-r-p*, as *slurp*, *sherbet*. An experiment carried out over ffity years ago found that people preferred to use the nonsense word *maluma* to label a rounded object, and *takete* to apply to a spiky one in several different countries, though there was no evidence of this preference in the words of the languages themselves. Long, polysyllabic words tend to be used to denote catastrophic events, for example *apocalyptic atrocity, cataclysmic abominations*, describing the New York 'twin towers' attack of 2001. A language may also develop idiosyncratic associations between sounds and events: English tends to favour words beginning with *fl-* for sporadic bursts of light, as *flash, flare, flicker*.

specific language impairment (SLI) Deviant or delayed language acquisition by a child who exhibits no other cognitive or neurological problems. Such impairments may affect different sub-sections of the language system.

speech act theory A claim that uttering language involves deeds, not mere words. For example, a sentence *I promise to come* is an act of promising, and a sentence *Are you coming?* is an act of questioning. The theory was proposed by the British philosopher J. L. Austin (1911–1960), and was further developed by the British philosopher J. R. Searle. It is an approach which is of interest to the interpretation of speech, since humans often use apparently inappropriate speech acts. For example, the question: *Aren't you tired?* might be intended as a command: *Go to bed.* It is therefore necessary to list the *felicity conditions* for each act (the background conditions which allow a person to identify which speech act is being performed). This approach to interpretation overlaps with that of the American philosopher Paul Grice, with his proposal for a **co-operative principle** which enables humans to interact successfully. (See also **interpretation; speech comprehension.**)

speech comprehension Understanding spoken language. This is a complex operation which can be divided into several overlapping processes: **speech perception** (identifying the sounds uttered), **word recognition** (deciding which word has been said), **parsing** (the assignment of structure to the words recognised) and **interpretation** (**assignment of meaning**):

SPEECH PERCEPTION - - - - - - - - - - - - - - - - - - - >
   WORD RECOGNITION - - - - - - - - - - - - - - - - - >
      PARSING - >
        INTERPRETATION - - - - - - - - - - - - - - - - - >

There is considerable disagreement over the extent to which these processes are interlinked or independent of one another. In writing and signing, the same overall processes occur, though the perception stage involves sight rather than hearing.

speech error see **slip of the tongue**

speech perception The identification of spoken sounds. This is the first of several overlapping processes in speech comprehension, though the term is sometimes used for the whole of speech understanding. Perceiving speech is an active process, in which a hearer reconstructs the probable sounds on the basis of outline clues. This is partly because normal speech is too fast for the human ear to register in detail, and partly because the acoustic signal (sound wave pattern) varies for each sound, in some cases overlapping with the pattern of other sounds (**acoustic variance**). There is considerable disagreement as to how the sounds perceived are fitted onto words in the early phases of word recognition (**lexical access**). In writing and signing, the recognition of letters and signs is equally complex. (See also **speech comprehension**.)

speech planning Outline preparation of speech. This is the first of several overlapping processes in producing speech. It involves deciding what to say, and making preliminary decisions about how to say it. Speech is probably planned in chunks consisting of *tone groups* (a stretch of speech with a single intonation contour). This information comes partly from studying **pauses**, but primarily from **slips of the tongue** (unintended speech errors), since errors which involve wrong assemblage normally occur within the tone group, as in *I'll hit that with you* (I'll hit you with that). (See also **speech production**.)

speech production Preparing and uttering speech. This involves several overlapping processes: **planning** (decision of what to say, and outline of how to say it), **word retrieval** (selecting and finding words), integration of words and syntax, uttering speech, monitoring output (checking what has been said).

PLANNING- >
   WORD RETRIEVAL - - - - - - - - - - - - - - - - - - >
      INTEGRATION OF WORDS AND SYNTAX- - >
         UTTERING SPEECH - - - - - - - - - - - - - - >
           MONITORING OUTPUT - - - - - - - - - - - >

Evidence for the various processes comes partly from **pauses**, but primarily from **slips of the tongue** (unintended errors), as in *interlapping* (interlinked + overlapping); *he wash upped* (washed up) *the dishes*; *lowing the morn* (mowing the lawn). Humans possibly gather together the ingredients required in some internal planning space, then organise them into the order required for speech, perhaps by a means of a **scan-copier**, a device which 'scans' and 'copies' each item. The whole production process is heavily dependent on stress and rhythm, which forms the framework for the output. A **monitoring device** checks the final output.

split brain A condition in which the two hemispheres (halves) of the brain have been separated, so that a patient has in effect two separate brains. Such an operation is occasionally carried out in order to control seizures in cases of severe epilepsy. From the language point of view, the interest of such a procedure lies in the fact that it is possible to test each brain hemisphere separately. Speech processing is carried out primarily in the left hemisphere, though some of these patients have been able to name objects when using only the right hemisphere, suggesting that linguistic operations such as simple naming could be carried out in either hemisphere. (See also **brain; localisation.**)

spoonerism The exchange of a pair of sounds, as in *Let's meet in the par cark* (car park), and *I must get these shoes holed and sealed* (soled and heeled). These errors are named after the Reverend A. Spooner (1844–1930), Dean and Warden of New College, Oxford around a century ago, who reputedly made errors, such as: *The cat jumped out of the window and popped on its drawers* (dropped on its paws) and *You will go home by the town drain* (down train). The errors reported to have been made by the original Spooner are somewhat improbable, and may have been inventions. But 'exchanges' (or *transpositions*) of sounds, syllables and words, are a fairly common type of **assemblage error.** These are **slips of the tongue** (speech errors) in which the correct items have been selected, but then wrongly assembled. Such errors can provide useful information about speech production. (See also **exchange error.**)

spreading activation model see **interactive activation model**

storage vs retrieval see **retrieval vs storage**

story grammar The underlying structure of a length of text (spoken or written). Humans have inbuilt expectations about how stories are constructed, in rather the same way as they have expectations about sentence structure. According to one theory, they expect stories to begin with a *setting*, then to involve several *episodes*, each of which is likely to be an *event* followed by the characters' *reactions* to it. There is some disagreement as to how best to write story grammars, but some study of how humans handle stretches longer than the sentence is essential. Story grammars are primarily an attempt to specify the likely structure of the story, rather than an account of how hearers identify this structure.

stranding error A speech error in which a word ending has become separated from the word it should have been attached to, as in *You must square it facely* (face it squarely), where -*ly* is apparently stranded. Unintended speech errors (**slips of the tongue**) provide important information about the process of speech production. In this case, a mistake has been made in the slotting together of words and syntax in a way which indicates that the rhythm of words is important, since *face it* and *squarely* have identical stress patterns. The switching over of *square* and *face* is a type of **assemblage error** known as an **exchange**. (See also **speech production**.)

structural ambiguity see **ambiguity**

structure-dependence Reliance on internal organisation. This is an important design feature of language. An utterance is not just a random collection of words, but a systematically organised whole. Its internal structure must be understood in order to handle the language adequately. For example, in a sentence such as *Felix chased the small brown mouse*, English speakers, possibly without realising it, treat *the small brown mouse* as a structural unit which can be switched around, or replaced by a substitute, as in *The small brown mouse was chased by Felix*; *Felix chased it*; *What did Felix chase?* Knowledge that language is structure-dependent may be genetically inbuilt in children. (See also **innateness**.)

subset principle see **overgeneralisation**

substitution errors see **selection errors**

suppression The blocking of unwanted words. Humans mentally consider numerous words in the processes of speech recognition and production, then narrow them down to the one required by suppressing the unwanted ones – though they are not usually aware of doing this. The **cohort model** is one theory which describes how this may happen. (See **overactivation**.)

surface dyslexia see **dyslexia**

surface structure see **transformational grammar**

surface structure ambiguity see **ambiguity**

switch setting see **parameter setting**

syntax see **grammar**

T

target An intended utterance. The term is found in discussions of **slips of the tongue** (unintended speech errors) where the word 'target' is used of the utterance at which the speaker was apparently aiming, as in: 'The target is hard to identify for the tongue slip *indulgement*'.

telegraphic speech Speech which contains mainly 'content' words and omits word endings and the 'little' words which link them together, so sounding superficially like a telegram or newspaper headline. It is characteristic of children at an early stage of acquisition, particularly the two-word stage, when they say things such as *Want milk*; *Mummy come*; *Car go*. It is also characteristic of a type of speech disorder known as **agrammatic aphasia**. However, the similarity between these two types of telegraphic speech is a superficial one only, although at one time supporters of the **regression hypothesis** argued that they were similar. (See also **two-word stage**.)

telescopic blends see **blend**

thematic roles The **semantic roles** played by words and groups of words in the mental lexicon. The word *theme* was originally envisaged as the entity which underwent some happening, for example THE ROCK in *THE ROCK rolled down the hill, David kicked THE ROCK*. The idea of thematic/semantic roles is found (with minor variations) in the proposals of various linguists, though the term 'thematic roles' is particularly associated with transformational-generative grammar, which has shortened it to *theta-roles* or *θ–roles*. Around ten are usually specified, though the exact number is disputed. Examples of commonly found theta-roles are ACTOR or AGENT, the initiator of some action, as *PETER kicked the rock*;

INSTRUMENT, the means by which something is done, as *Peter kicked the rock WITH HIS FOOT*. A problem which sometimes arises is that of distinguishing between roles: *Mary* in *MARY was given some flowers* might be regarded as a GOAL, the intended destination of the flowers, or as a BENEFACTIVE, the enitity which benefits from an action. Some theories allow a word to have more than one semantic role.

theory of mind see **mind, theory of**

theta roles see **thematic roles**

thought and language The extent to which language and thought are separate or interwoven is a much-disputed topic. The **Sapir–Whorf hypothesis** proposed a strong form of linguistic relativity, arguing that a person's language fundamentally affected his or her thoughts. This is now assumed to be untenable in its most extreme formulation, though is partially borne out in a number of domains, such as gender and colour. Most people assume that linguistic ability is to some extent separate from thought, as is shown by rare cases of children suffering from **chatterbox syndrome**. Such children talk fluently, but do not make sense.

tip-of-the-tongue state see **TOT phenomenon**

tone groups see **speech planning**

tongue-slip laws Recurring patterns found in **slips of the tongue** (unintended speech errors). These regularities are somewhat loosely referred to as 'laws'. For example, 'Errors normally fit in with the syllable structure of the language being spoken'. Therefore an error such as *stee* *franding* (free standing) is probable, but one such as *ftee sranding* is most unlikely , since *ft* and *sr* are not possible word-beginning sequences in English (an asterisk indicates an impossible sequence). Such 'laws' enable researchers to draw conclusions about **speech production.**

top-down vs bottom-up processing A controversy as to whether humans comprehend sentences by imposing an outline structure on them, or by assembling together pieces. The terms 'top' and 'bottom' refer to the top and bottom of a linguistic tree (see Fig. 5). In a top-down approach, the hearer would subconsciously say: 'Look for an NP (noun phrase = phrase containing a noun), followed by a VP (verb phrase = phrase containing a verb)'. In a bottom-up approach, the hearer would subconsciously say 'Gather up the words, and check if they can be assembled in any useful way'. According to some psycholinguists, both processes may be going on at once. (See also **speech comprehension.**)

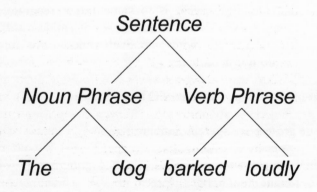

Fig. 5   Linguistic tree

TOT phenomenon The common experience in which a person feels that an elusive word is on the 'tip-of-the-tongue' (TOT). This phenomenon can provide important information about how words are stored and retrieved from the mind, because the searcher can often remember some information about the 'missing' word, and can propose similar-sounding and similar-meaning words. For example, the psychologist Sigmund Freud claimed (1901) that when searching for *Monaco* (whose capital is Monte Carlo) the substitute words Piedmont, Montevideo, Colico, and Montenegro came to mind. In a famous experiment in 1966, two American psychologists, Roger Brown and David McNeill, read out definitions of relatively uncommon words to students, and then quizzed those in a TOT state. They showed that people could remember the beginnings of words better than the ends, and the ends better than the middle. They could also often remember the number of syllables, suggesting that these facets of the word are more clearly 'inked in' in the mind than some others. (See also **speech production; word retrieval**.)

transformational grammar A theory about language which suggests that there are two levels of structure, *deep structure* and *surface structure*, linked by processes known as 'transformations'. For example, in the sentence: *What can Marigold take?* English speakers subconsciously know that *take* is a verb which must have an object (you cannot say: **Marigold took*), and that this object is *what*. A transformational grammar 'captures' this, by suggesting that at a deeper level, the order of the components is: *Marigold can take what?*. A transformation then brings *what* to the front. The theory was proposed by the American linguist Noam **Chomsky**, and over the years has been altered considerably. Throughout its history, psycholinguists have been interested in testing whether a transformational grammar has any **psychological reality**. Many early experiments were misleading, because they were often based on mistaken assumptions. Transformational grammar has never claimed to represent the steps by which speakers produce or comprehend sentences. Instead, it merely claims to represent, in an indirect way, the relationships between sentences which exist in the minds of speakers. Recent versions also claim to encapsulate a human's innate linguistic endowment, in the form of **Universal Grammar**. (See also **correspondence hypothesis; derivational theory of complexity; innateness**.)

transposition see **exchange error; spoonerism**

troponymy A relationship between verbs and their subordinates, coined from the Greek words *tropos* 'way' and *onoma* 'name' by George Miller and his associates in the electronic dictionary **WordNet**. A superordinate verb such as *talk* has subordinates such as *babble, lisp, stutter*, all meaning 'to talk in a particular way.'

turn-taking The characteristic of taking it in turns to talk. This appears to be innate in humans, but is rare among animals – though is found in the so-called **antiphonal singing** of some bird species.

two-word stage A point in child language development when children start putting two words together, as in *Hi mommy; Allgone milk; Want cookie*. This typically comes after several months of uttering single words, and is usually reached at around eighteen months, though there is considerable variation from child to child. A few children seem to miss this stage out, instead producing **scribble talk**, longish indistinct utterances with good intonation patterns, but with only occasional identifiable words. In the early 1960s, children were thought to have a universal pattern underlying two-word utterances, known as a **pivot grammar**, but later work showed this claim to be unjustified. Two-word utterances turn out to be similar in content all round the world, with children expressing meanings such as, for example PLACE (*Birdie chair* 'the bird's on the chair'), RECURRENCE (*Nother bee* 'there's another bee'), and POSSESSION (*Daddy shoe* 'that's daddy's shoe'). There is considerable argument as to whether these early utterances represent the consistent expression of various types of meaning, or whether the child can be said to have a primitive grammar. An influential viewpoint is that of the American psychologist Martin Braine, who proposed (1976) that children use **limited scope formulae**, patterns which relate to small areas of language, and which are initially based on meaning relations. However, this leaves undecided the question of how children move over to a proper grammatical system, something which is still under discussion. One recent proposal involves **bootstrapping**, the claim that children, like some computers, require a preliminary 'booting' or 'bootstrapping' procedure to get them going, before they move on to the real thing.

U

UG see **Universal Grammar**

undergeneralisation see **overgeneralisation**

uniqueness principle The principle of 'one form, one meaning'. This tendency is found strongly among children, who resist allowing something to have more than one name. For example, a child might dispute the fact that a *horse* is an *animal*, on the grounds that it is a *horse*. The uniqueness principle is one way in which children may correct their mistakes. For example, if a child says *taked*, and then later hears an adult say *took*, he or she may reconsider the form *taked*, on the grounds that there are unlikely to be two forms which mean the same. The uniqueness principle is also known as the *principle of contrast*.

Universal Grammar (UG) Genetically programmed information about language, according to the American linguist Noam **Chomsky**. In his opinion, every child is innately pre-programmed with information about universal language principles. For example, in a sentence such as *Otto ate six small apples and four large pears*, children would instinctively know that it is impossible to split the object noun phrase (phrase containing a noun), and bring only part of it to the front, saying * *Which apples did Otto eat and four large pears?* (with an asterisk marking an impossible sentence). In addition, children would be pre-wired with a number of possible options available to language, which need to be selected after exposure to their own language. In Chomsky's words, they need to 'set the parameters' (fix the necessary options). Together, the principles and parameters make up **Universal Grammar**. Chomsky's proposals are fairly controversial, and are an attempt to solve the **learnability** problem, the fact that children acquire language more efficiently and easily than one might expect, given the evidence available to them: they therefore may have some outline knowledge of what language is like in advance. (See also **parameter setting**.)

uptake vs input see **input vs uptake**

usage vs knowledge see **knowledge vs usage**

V

veiled controlled processes Speech comprehension processes in which the person comprehending is unaware of the processes he or she is carrying out. At one time, psychologists distinguished between automatic processes, such as hearing a nearby noise, and controlled processes, such as actively identifying the source of the noise. A third type, veiled controlled processes, are those for which psycholinguists have found evidence of active human attention, but of which the speaker is unaware. For example, hearers are thought to subconsciously notice more types of **ambiguity** than they consciously realise.

verbal complexity hypothesis A suggestion that **speech comprehension** is affected by the number of constructions associated with a particular verb. A verb such as *expect* should therefore be harder to comprehend than one such as *write*. This hypothesis does not seem to be supported. In general, comprehension of verbs is complicated only in cases where it is unclear who is doing what to whom, and when infrequently used constructions are found.

vervet monkey A species of African monkey whose alarm calls distinguish between different types of enemy: a *chutter* signifies a snake, causing other monkeys to stand on their hind legs, and inspect the ground; a *rraup* warns of an attack from an eagle, upon which the monkeys dive down and hide among the vegetation; a *chirp* indicates a lion or leopard, causing the monkeys to leap up any nearby tree. This system could represent an early stage in the use of arbitrary symbols for communication, according to those who believe that human language evolved directly out of an earlier animal communication system (continuity theory). (See also **continuity vs discontinuity theories**.)

vocabulary see **mental lexicon**

vocabulary size The vocabulary size of an educated adult English native speaker is thought to be at least 50,000 words. The size is normally estimated by testing a dictionary sample, though care has to be taken, as the sampling may be misleading, due partly to the **big dictionary effect**.

Vygotsky, L. S. (1893–1934) Russian psychologist, who was particularly concerned with child development. His notion of a **chain complex** was especially influential, in which various meanings of a word are presumed to be chained on to one another by association.

$$\boxed{W}$$

Washoe The name of a female chimp, who was born in county Washoe in Nevada. She was the first of a number of chimps to learn a simplified **sign language**. She showed clearly that chimps are able to use signs as symbols. For example, she used the sign for *key* to refer to several different keys, and could generalise it to new keys. She was also able to be creative, by combining signs in a novel way, as in *Go sweet* 'Please take me to the raspberry bushes'. However, it is not clear that she ever developed any genuine rules of grammar. One problem in deciding this is that chimps often repeat signs, so analysing their output presents a number of difficulties. More recently, she is reported to have taught a number of single signs to her adopted child chimp, Loulis. (See also **ape signing**.)

Wernicke's aphasia see **fluent aphasia**

Wernicke's area An area of the brain named after the German neurologist Carl Wernicke, who published a paper in 1874, pointing out that an area towards the back of the left side of the brain (technically, the first temporal gyrus) seemed to be important for understanding speech. Wernicke's discovery that posterior (back) regions of the brain are important for speech comprehension complemented an earlier discovery, usually attributed to the Frenchman Paul Broca, that certain anterior (front) portions of the brain are important for speech production. However, the exact localisation of speech processes is a matter of some dispute. (See also **brain; Broca's area; localisation.**)

Whorfian hypothesis see **Sapir–Whorf hypothesis**

Williams' syndrome A neurological disorder in which sufferers lack spatial awareness, yet can speak fluently. When asked to draw an object, patients typically draw small sections of it, which they are unable to assemble together into a whole. In contrast, they can describe their thoughts and feelings in a coherent and well-organised way. The importance of such cases is that they show that certain cognitive abilities may be separated out within the mind.

word association The linking of one word with another in the mind. Word associations are discovered by asking a question such as 'What is the first word you think of when I say *sun*?' and then noting the response, which will be, perhaps, *moon* or *heat* or *summer*. Such experiments are useful in outline, but they still leave numerous questions unanswered, such as the different types of link which exist between words. Typically, adults give responses which involve the same *word class* (part of speech), as with *sun* (noun) leading to *moon* (noun), or *dark* (adjective) to *light* (adjective). Children tend to respond with a likely neighbour, as with *dark* leading to *night* (*dark night*), or *sun* to *shine* (*sunshine, the sun shines*). Such differences suggest that children may have words organised differently in their mind from adults.

word class see **word association**

word finding see **word retrieval**

word-initial cohort see **cohort model**

WordNet An electronic lexical database developed at Princeton University by George Miller and his colleagues. Its importance lies in that it has considerable 'psychological reality', particularly in that it recognises that humans treat different word classes (parts of speech) differently from one another.

word recognition Identifying a word in **speech comprehension** or reading. This is only one of a number of overlapping processes in understanding language. Word recognition possibly involves two interlinked stages: first, **lexical access,** in which the sounds are matched against probable words; secondly, narrowing down of the multiple possibilities to one single word. There are various theories as to how this is done. Influential models of word recognition are the **cohort model, interactive activation models,** and (earlier on) the **logogen model.**

word retrieval Selecting and finding words in **speech production.** This is only one of a number of overlapping processes in producing speech. **Selection errors,** a type of **slip of the tongue** (unintended speech error), provide important information about this process, as in *Your objections* *are frivial* (frivolous + trivial) and *He led a scientific exhibition* (expedition). The **tip-of-the-tongue phenomenon** (the state in which people searching for a word claim that it is 'on the tip of their tongue') also provides useful clues. Recent theories of word retrieval suggest that the human mind contemplates a variety of words, then narrows these down to the one finally selected. Exactly how this happens is unclear: an **interactive activation model** of the process is plausible.

word salad A confusing jumble of words, as is typically produced by some patients suffering from a mental disorder such as schizophrenia. Superficially, the words are haphazard. But on closer inspection, some of the links can be explained, as in: *I had a little goldfish too, like a clown. Happy Hallowe'en down*; people dress up as clowns at Hallowe'en, and *clown* rhymes with *down*. They indicate that the patient's mind may be overexcited, and making too many associations, which cannot be suppressed. Such salads may therefore be an uncontrolled form of the normal process of word finding, where more words are likely to be activated than are actually required. (See also **word retrieval**.)

working memory (also sometimes referred to as *short-term memory*) A somewhat ambiguous term, used with different meanings in books on psychology. Within psycholinguistics, most researchers use it to refer to the amount of speech that can be kept in a person's mind when planning or interpreting an utterance.

wug test An experiment for checking on children's ability to add word endings to nonsense words, devised by the American Jean Berko-Gleason (1958). The first item was a picture of a small birdlike creature, with the information: 'This is a wug'. Underneath were two more wugs, with the note: 'Now there is another one. There are two of them. There are two . . . ?' Children who said *wugs* showed that they had a **rule** for forming plurals in English. The 'wug test' went on to ask about other items, such as the past tenses of verbs. This type of experiment is important, because it shows that children are acquiring their own linguistic system, and are not just imitating adult forms, since they had presumably never come across a wug before.

Suggestions for Further Reading

These reading suggestions are listed under:
1. Introductory reading (easy to read)
2. Basic text books (straightforward textbooks)
3. Books of readings (various writers)

The books are listed in alphabetical order of author within each section, accompanied by a brief comment about each book.

1. Introductory reading

Aitchison, Jean (2003) *Words in the mind: An introduction to the mental lexicon* (3rd edn), Oxford: Basil Blackwell. How people store words in their minds, and find the ones they need when producing and understanding speech.

Aitchison, Jean (1998) *The articulate mammal: An introduction to psycholinguistics* (4th edn), London: Unwin Hyman. An overview of how humans acquire, comprehend and produce speech.

Aitchison, Jean (1997) *The language web: The power and problem of words*, Cambridge: Cambridge University Press. An introduction to various facets of language, including child language, memory for words, and whether language affects thought.

Aitchison, Jean (1996: Canto edition: 2000) *The seeds of speech: Language origin and evolution*, Cambridge: Cambridge University Press. How language began, and how it developed and spread around the world.

Altman, Gerry T. M. (1997) *The ascent of Babel: An exploration of language, mind, and understanding*, Oxford: Oxford University Press. A general introduction by a specialist in language and the brain.

Calvin, William A. (1996) *The celebral code: Thinking a thought in the mosaics of the mind*, Cambridge, MA: MIT Press. An introductory book which looks into the relationship between language and thought.

Chiat, Shula (2000) *Understanding children with language problems*, Cambridge: Cambridge University Press. A brief, clear introduction to what can go wrong when acquiring language.

Crystal, David (1986) *Listen to your child*, Harmondsworth, Middlesex: Penguin. An easy-to-read introduction to child language development, primarily written for parents.

Gardner, Howard (1975) *The shattered mind*, New York: Knopf. Outdated in places, but still a fascinating account of the results of damage to the brain, including chapters on aphasia.

Grant, Linda (1998) *Remind me who I am, again*, London: Granta Books. Linda Grant's mother suffered from MID (multi-infarct dementia). A sad and amusing account of the problems encountered by her mother, whose short-term memory was virtually obliterated.

Hale, Sheila (2002) *The man who lost his language*, London: Allen Lane. The historian Sir John Hale suffered a massive stroke, age 68, which resulted in anosognosia, unawareness of his problems: he endlessly repeated the phrase *da woah* with varied intonation, apparently thinking he was conversing normally. A fascinating account by his wife of her attempts to understand her husband's bizarre behaviour.

Obler, Loraine K. and Kris Gjerlow (1999) *Language and the brain*, Cambridge: Cambridge University Press. A clear overview of what we know about the organisation of language in the brain, and what can go wrong.

Pinker, Steven (1994) *The language instinct: The new science of language and mind*, London: Allen Lane. An easy-to-read view of language, highlighting the fact that it is an instinct inbuilt in humans.

Pinker, Steven (1999) *Words and rules: The ingredients of language*, London: Weidenfeld and Nicolson. A look at the relationships between words, and the rules which link them together.

Posner, Michael I. and Marcus E. Raichle (1994) *Images of mind*, NY: W. H. Freeman. A clear, and superbly illustrated book on the human brain.

Rée, Jonathan (1999) *I see a voice: Language, deafness and the senses – a philosophical history*, London: Harper Collins. An overview of past approaches to deafness, and the slow progress of understanding and educating the deaf.

Shenk, David (2002) *The forgetting: Understanding Alzheimer's: A biography of a disease*, London: Harper Collins. A clear account of the early, middle, and late stages of Alzheimer's disease. Among the cases discussed are those of Ronald Reagan and Jonathan Swift.

Snowling, Margaret (1987) *Dyslexia: A cognitive developmental perspective*, Oxford: Blackwell. A clear overview.

Springer, Sally P. and Georg Deutsch (1993) *Left brain, right brain* (4th edn), New York: Springer. A readable introduction to the brain.

2. Basic text books

Bloom, Paul (2000) *How children learn the meanings of words*, Cambridge, MA: MIT Press. A thoughtful discussion of a key issue.

Bond, Zinny S. (1999) *Slips of the ear: Errors in the perception of casual conversation*, London: Academic Press. Multiple examples of how people perceive, and misperceive what they hear.

Boysson-Bardies, Bénédicte de (1999) *How language comes to children: from birth to two years*, Cambridge, MA: MIT Press. A careful overview of the early months and years.

Caplan, David (1992) *Language: Structure, processing and disorders*, Cambridge, MA: MIT Press. A fact-packed introduction to language written by a neurolinguist.

Chomsky, Noam (2000) *New horizons in the study of language and mind*, Cambridge: Cambridge University Press. Edited interviews and discussions: a useful overview of some of Chomsky's recent ideas.

Clark, Andy (1997) *Being there: Putting brain, body and world together again*, Cambridge, MA: MIT Press. A wide-ranging overview of the human brain and mind, and the way they fit together in recent thought.

Clark, Eve V. (1993) *The lexicon in acquisition*, Cambridge: Cambridge University Press. A detailed survey of how children acquire word meanings.

Cotterill, Rodney (1998) *Enchanted looms: Conscious networks in brains and computers*, Cambridge: Cambridge University Press. A wide-ranging introduction to the brain.

Gathercole, Susan E. and Alan D. Baddeley (1993) *Working memory and language*, Hove, East Sussex: Lawrence Erlbaum Associates. The role of working memory in language processing, bringing together findings from normal adults, brain-damaged patients, and children.

Gopnik, Alison and Andrew Meltzoff (1997) *Words, thoughts and theories*, Cambridge, MA: MIT Press. A look at young children's understanding of word meaning.

Jusczyk, Peter W. (1997) *The discovery of spoken language*, Cambridge, MA: MIT Press. A book which pays attention to the very early stages in child language, in particular how babies learn to segment utterances and identify sounds.

Karmiloff, Kyra and Annette Karmiloff-Smith (2001) *Pathways to language: From fetus to adolescent*, Cambridge, MA: MIT Press. An overview of child language development, starting with what the child can hear when in the womb.

Lieberman, Philip (1998) *Eve spoke: Human language and human evolution*, London: Picador. The origin of language, with particular attention to the physical properties of brains and skulls.

Taylor, John R. (1995) *Linguistic categorization: Prototypes in linguistic theory* (2nd edn), Oxford: Clarendon. How humans put words into categories: a useful exploration of prototype theory.

3. Books of readings

Berko-Gleason, Jean (ed.) (1993) *The development of language* (3rd edn), New York: Charles Merrill. How children acquire language, written by a variety of experts.

Berko-Gleason, Jean and Nan Bernstein Ratner (eds) (1998) *Psycholinguistics* (2nd edn), Orlando, FL: Harcourt Brace. A wide-ranging introduction, written by a number of well-known scholars in the field.

Bloom, Paul (ed.) (1994) *Language acquisition: Core readings*, Cambridge, MA: MIT Press. Various key readings written in the past twenty years.

Bowerman, Melissa and Stephen C. Levinson (eds) (2001) *Language acquisition and conceptual development*, Cambridge: Cambridge University Press. An exploration of various cultures, some of which are quite different from English, showing that a child's physical environment has a great influence on how the world is perceived.

Brown, Gillian, Kirsten Malmkjaer, Alastair Pollitt and John Williams (eds) (1994) *Language and understanding*, Oxford: Oxford University Press. A variety of introductory papers by various people on this key topic.

Degraff, Michel (ed.) (1999) *Language creation and language change: Creolization, diachrony and development*, Cambridge, MA: MIT Press. As the title suggests, an attempt to bring together writings on child language, creole languages and language change.

Dupoux, Emmanuel (ed.) (2001) *Language, brain and cognitive development*, (Cambridge, MA: MIT Press). A range of papers in honour of Jacques Mehler, one of the major figures in the field of psycholinguistics.

Fletcher, Paul and Brian MacWhinney (eds) (1995) *The handbook of child language*, Oxford: Blackwell. A massive volume (almost 800 pages) on almost every aspect of child language, including non-normal development, by twenty-five writers/academics.

Gallaway, Clare and Brian J. Richards (eds) (1994) *Input and interaction in language acquisition*, Cambridge: Cambridge University Press. Discusses the facts and controversies surrounding talk to children.

Gleitman, Lila R. and Mark Liberman (1995) *Language: An invitation to cognitive science*, vol. 1 (2nd edn), Cambridge, MA: MIT Press. An overview with contributions by a number of key figures in the field.

Hyltenstam, Kenneth and Ake Viberg (eds) (1993). *Progression and regression in language: Sociocultural, neuropsychological and linguistic perspectives*, Cambridge: Cambridge University Press. Explores changes in the language of societies and individuals which involve both gain or loss in linguistic complexity.

Miller, Joanne L. and Peter D. Eimas (eds) (1995) *Speech, language and communication* (2nd edn), London: Academic Press. Ten careful and fairly lengthy papers by experts in the field.